WINNING RACQUETBALL

Skills, Drills, and Strategies

Ed Turner, PhD
Appalachian State University

Woody Clouse
International Racquetball Tour Professional

Human Kinetics

Library of Congress Cataloging-in-Publication Data

Turner, Edward T.
  Winning racquetball : skills, drills, and strategies / Ed Turner,
Woody Clouse.
    p.   cm.
  Rev. ed. of: Skills & strategies for winning racquetball. c1988.
  Includes bibliographical references and index.
  ISBN 0-87322-721-2 (paper)
    1. Racquetball. I. Clouse, Woody, 1965-   . II. Turner, Edward
T. Skills & strategies for winning racquetball. III. Title.
  GV1003.34.T87   1995
  796.34'3--dc20   95-13029
                                                                  CIP
  ISBN: 0-87322-721-2

Developmental Editor: Rodd Whelpley; **Assistant Editor:** Kent Reel; **Editorial Assistant:** Andrew Starr; **Copyeditor:** Bob Replinger; **Proofreader:** Pam Johnson; **Indexer:** Joan Griffitts; **Typesetters:** Ruby Zimmerman and Tara Welsch; **Text Designer:** Stuart Cartwright; **Layout:** Tara Welsch and Ruby Zimmerman; **Cover Designer:** Jack Davis; **Photographer (cover):** Corneilus Photography; **Photographer (interior):** Robert Caldwell except where noted; **Illustrator:** Tara Welsch; **Printer:** Sierra Printers, Inc.

Human Kinetics books are available at special discounts for bulk purchase. Special editions or book excerpts can also be created to specification. For details, contact the Special Sales Manager at Human Kinetics.

Printed in the United States of America   10   9   8   7   6   5   4   3   2   1

Human Kinetics
P.O. Box 5076, Champaign, IL 61825-5076
1-800-747-4457

Canada: Human Kinetics, Box 24040, Windsor, ON N8Y 4Y9
1-800-465-7301 (in Canada only)

Europe: Human Kinetics, P.O. Box IW14, Leeds LS16 6TR, United Kingdom
(44) 1132 781708

Australia: Human Kinetics, 2 Ingrid Street, Clapham 5062, South Australia
(08) 371 3755

New Zealand: Human Kinetics, P.O. Box 105-231, Auckland 1
(09) 523 3462

To Paul Renz, George Kramer, and to Luke and Matt, who both have made life a pleasure.

—Ed Turner

To my wife, Jacqueline, who has been the stability and support to make my professional racquetball a reality.

—Woody Clouse

Lastly, to the racquetball players of the world, thanks.

Contents

Preface

We love racquetball. We love thinking about it, talking about it, reading about it, writing about it. But most of all, we love playing it and playing it well. That's why we're drawn to racquetball, both as competitors and as teachers. Whether you've been playing for years or whether you've just discovered the sport, if you share our passion, this book is for you. We pooled our 30 years of playing and teaching knowledge to create this book. With *Winning Racquetball* we offer you a practical guide to get more from your workouts, to improve your game, and to have more fun in the process.

We've divided *Winning Racquetball* into three parts: Preparing to Play, Mastering Skills and Strategies, and Competing. Preparing to Play discusses topics such as equipment and facilities selection; conditioning and safety; and determining your current skill level. Mastering Skills and Strategies focuses on grips, power supplies, hitting position, types of shots, volleys, serves, return of serves, diving, movement patterns, footwork, anticipation, half-volleys, and playing the angles. The chapters in Part III, Competing, explore the mental aspects of the game, help you prepare for tournament competition, introduce you to doubles, and give you a glimpse into life as a touring professional.

We've packed the book with photos and figures that demonstrate proper execution and illustrate sound strategies. Each chapter has special features that give you quick references for improving your game: The key elements highlight the most important parts of each skill we present; drill sections at the end of chapters show you how best to groove the new skills you'll pick up; and Woody has provided tips throughout the text specifically designed to help you take your game to its highest level. Appendix A is a mini clinic that describes the 13 most common errors made in racquetball and how to correct them.

Our goal was to write the book we'd always hoped to read. That's why we've made *Winning Racquetball* the most comprehensive book on racquetball we know of. We want *Winning Racquetball* to take center court in your racquetball library; we hope you'll read it, enjoy it, use it, practice, and then step into the court to play winning racquetball.

—Ed Turner
Woody Clouse

*A*cknowledgments

Thanks to photographer Bob Caldwell and his wife, Sharon, for the majority of the photos in the text. Thanks also to *KILLSHOT* magazine for their help in making this text possible. Lastly, a special thanks to Carla Tobia for the final typing of this manuscript and to Candy Adkins for being so photogenic.

Key to Diagrams

H = Hitter

O = Opponent

L = Left

R = Right or Receiver

S = Server

B = Bounce

X = Player

● = Ball

– – – – = Path of ball

🐾 = Foot placement

RHO = Right-handed opponent

LHO = Left-handed opponent

C = Ceiling

FW = Front wall

SW = Side wall

Part I

PREPARING TO PLAY

Chapter 1

Choosing Equipment and Facilities

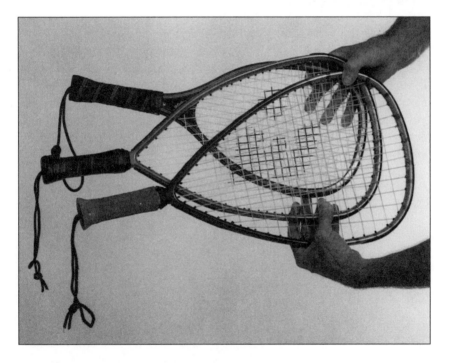

*T*hree general rules dictate equipment selection:

1. Individual preference. Do you like a head-heavy racquet or one that is evenly weighted?
2. The type and style of your game. Are you a power or finesse player? Do you frustrate opponents with your garbage shots or do you steadily work for kills?

3. Your skill level. As a beginner, do you really want that expensive graphite racquet?

Equipment is constantly being changed and improved. To be sure, many new items will be introduced to the market after this book is in print, but if you use the information provided in this chapter and purchase with sound reasoning, you will obtain usable, quality equipment that fits your needs.

RACQUETS AND GRIPS

You must consider size, grip, shape, price, manufacturer, weight, material, and string qualities when selecting your racquet. Your racquet should also have sweet spots that feel right for you. Each of these considerations is important in selecting the racquet best suited for your type, style, and level of play. Before purchasing a racquet, you should know the names of the parts so you'll be better able to appreciate the differences between models the salesperson will show you (see Figure 1.1).

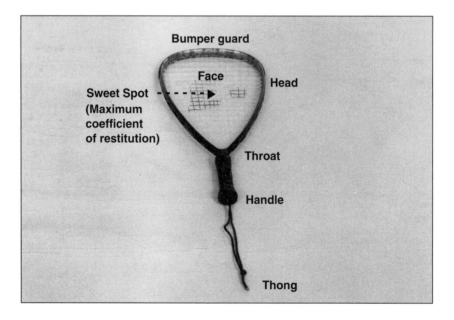

Figure 1.1   Racquet terminology.

Racquet Size

Larger racquets with a wide head or a wide body are more forgiving when you hit balls off center—the racquet doesn't twist in your hand as much. Therefore, the larger the racquet head, the more stability you'll have. A longer racquet gives you more power and reach, but you lose some control. The variance of one and one quarter inches does not make an appreciable playing difference for most beginning or intermediate-level racquetball players, but it does significantly affect play at the advanced level. Rules prohibit racquets over 21 inches long. Today all racquets are either oversized or midsized.

Getting a Grip—Size, Shape, and Materials

The most important aspect of racquet size is the size of the grip (the circumference of the grip measured in inches and fractions of inches). Newcomers to racquetball, especially those who have played tennis, tend to select too large a grip. In tennis, large grips help maintain wrist stability. However, there's more wrist action in racquetball, so you'll want a smaller grip. Sizes range from 3-5/8 inches (super small), to 3-7/8 inches (extra small), to 4-1/8 inches (small). Some companies make a 3-3/4 inch grip size, and some racquets have a flared grip that tapers from smaller at the top to larger at the bottom.

The surest technique to determine your grip size is to use varying sizes until you find the one that feels best. A rule of thumb is that a smaller grip is best for individuals who need extra power and who have a small- to average-sized hand. Generally, the smaller your racquet grip, the more flexion-rotation, or wrist-snap, you can muster, thus increasing your power. The proper grip size is important in controlling your racquet. An improper grip size can cause the racquet handle to turn in your hand, bringing about a loss of control. As shown in Figure 1.2, a correct size grip, for most players, permits the ring finger to almost touch the base of the thumb.

The standard material for grips has long been leather, but within the last few years synthetic grips have been introduced. The synthetics have all the qualities of leather and are marketed as being less affected by perspiration. It is claimed that they can be gripped more tightly and provide more control without slippage. In both leather and synthetic grips, you'll want a tacky or sticky feeling. Usually, the less expensive the grip, the less tacky it feels. Leather grips should be

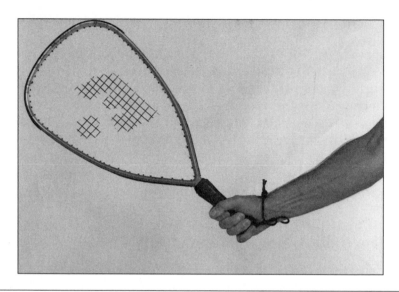

Figure 1.2   With the correct grip size your ring finger almost touches the base of your thumb.

made of top-quality leather and should be perforated with small holes to increase perspiration absorption. Today's rubber sleeve grips give a great long-lasting non-slip grip and are highly recommended.

Grips may either be flat or have raised ridges spiraling around the handle. The raised spiral gives the hitter a rougher surface, which allows for a firmer grasp. One problem with the raised spiral is that you'll wear it down in a particular pattern if you are consistent with your grip. Then, during play, if you don't get your fingers into the worn grooves you'll feel uncomfortable. In spite of this, some players prefer the raised spiral grip.

Racquet Shape

When racquetball first began, all racquets were oval- or round-headed. Today, many differently shaped racquets are available, but most racquet heads fall between teardrop and rectangular shapes. The head shape determines to some degree the location of the center of percussion (or sweet spot), size and shape of the sweet spot, flexibility of the racquet, torque of the racquet, and the ease with which you can return balls along the walls.

Different head shapes (as shown in Figure 1.3), along with the other factors listed in this chapter, dictate the actual state of the majority of these aforementioned factors. Head shape alone improves the ease with which one can return balls along the wall (wallpaper shots) or low to the floor. The flatter the sides and top of a racquet head, the more string surface the player can get closer to the floor or wall; therefore, the player gets more racquet surface on more balls when the balls are hugging the walls or floors.

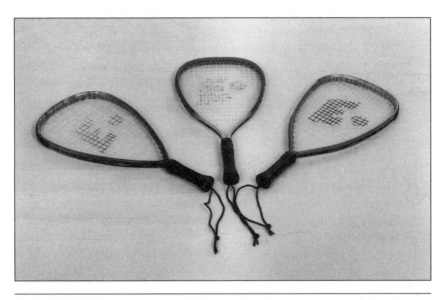

Figure 1.3   Today most racquets fall somewhere between rectangular and teardrop shaped.

Racquet frames have also changed in head thickness with both wide-bodied racquets and various tapered frames available. Changing the thickness of the frame offers both more power and more control.

Today's racquets are also stiffer than racquets of the past. A stiffer racquet allows both more control and more power. But, be careful; stiff racquets strung at a high tension can cause sore elbows and arms. Some racquet heads are tapered to provide a varying amount of stiffness throughout the frame to allow for tighter stringing and to deter arm and elbow soreness.

Racquet heads now range in size from 85 square inches to 115 square inches.

Price and Manufacturer

As racquetball has become more sophisticated, so has the equipment. Ektelon was the first company to manufacture only racquetball equipment, and they helped develop the production of sophisticated racquets. There are a large number of companies—including E-Force, Ektelon, Kennex Hogan, Head, Spalding, Wilson, Estca, Richcraft, and Transition—that offer a fine selection of quality racquets.

There are also many companies that manufacture racquets with little emphasis on quality control and therefore sell their products much more cheaply than brand-name racquets. We suggest that you buy a brand-name product to help ensure quality. Prices range from $25 to $300 for quality racquets. You can purchase other racquets from $10 on up.

Materials and Weight

The original racquet was wooden. Today, racquets are made of aluminum, or they are graphite-fiberglass-ceramic-boron-Kevlar composites. Obviously, if you buy a racquet made of cheap material, the chances of its lasting a reasonable length of time are slight. The life of the racquet also depends on how hard you hit the ball, how often you play, and how often you hit the walls and floor with the racquet.

To withstand the constant impacts of racquetball play, quality aluminum racquets should be in the 5,000-, 6,000-, or 7,000-series grade. The extruded form, or special shape, into which the aluminum is molded gives strength to the aluminum and thus to the racquet. If you were to cut through the aluminum in a racquet head, the cross-section would be in the design shape of the extrusion process, such as H-shaped or I-shaped. There are I beam, H beam, A beam, channel, flat channel, and flat I beam extrusions on the market. Today's aluminum racquets are designed primarily for beginners.

Intermediate to expert players generally choose a pricey graphite or composite racquet. Graphite has become popular because it is strong and lightweight and can be stiff or flexible depending on the materials with which it is combined. Some of the materials that are mixed with graphite to form composites are fiberglass, boron, Kevlar, nylon, ceramic, and carbon. Most of the qualities of each material can be manufactured into other materials; thus metal or composite racquets can be made to be durable, flexible or stiff, light or heavy.

Since the beginning of racquetball, the racquet has become progressively lighter, and today racquets weigh from 195 to 245 grams. A range of 195 to 225 grams is considered a light racquet, and 230 to 245 grams is a medium-weight racquet. In general, the lighter the racquet, the more control a player has, but with decreased weight some power is lost.

The balance of the racquet is also a consideration. Most racquets balance evenly from the head to the handle, but some are heavier in the head. A head-heavy racquet gives more power, but it also takes more strength to control. Base your choice of balance on personal preference.

Composite racquets must be kept out of the extreme heat that might be found in a tightly closed automobile trunk or interior. Temperatures in these areas may reach 140°F and this can cause your racquet to warp and your strings to stretch. Very cold temperatures also affect the playability of composite racquets; keep your racquet in an environment of 60°-80°F.

As racquetball continues to grow, new racquet models are constantly introduced to the market. Most of these are untested over long periods of time, and many new "ingenious" racquets are sold for a short time. So, don't assume a new high-tech racquet is an improvement. Find out how players who have used the new racquet feel about it, and play with any new racquet to see how it feels before you purchase it.

String Characteristics

Strings, like other parts of the racquet, have undergone much change. Strings are made from either nylon or gut. Strings with special textures, thickness, and resiliency are designed specifically for racquetball. Gauge indicates the thickness of the string; the higher the gauge, the thinner the string. Most racquets are strung with 16- or 17-gauge strings, which provide the best all-around hitting resiliency for most racquets. The thinner the string, say 17-gauge versus 16-gauge, the more elastic it is. The problem with a thinner string is that it is not as strong as a thicker string; 16-gauge string will last longer than 17-gauge string, but it will not be as resilient. Also available is 18-gauge string. Racquet strings stretch over a period of time, and this decrease in tension will be accompanied by a decrease in resiliency. Nylon strings take many forms, from standard monofilament to graphite-impregnated to square strings. Gut strings, which are made from the intestines of cattle, pigs, and sheep, have changed little over the years. Gut gives a more resilient rebound action on the ball than does nylon, but it's much more expensive.

String tension is also an important factor. The lower range is 24 to 30 pounds, and the higher range is 35 to 45 pounds. All other factors being equal, the looser the strings, the more power and the less control the player has. Increased string tension causes a decrease in the amount of time the ball stays in contact with the string, so you lose some control with tighter strings. Tighter strings also increase the amount of shock to your arm and hand.

Stringing patterns have changed from the standard, evenly spaced vertical and horizontal string pattern to new patterns, including geodesic string patterns, wishbone patterns, sunburst patterns, and denser stringing patterns on part or all of the string surface. If strings are spaced farther apart, they play as if they were at a lower tension. If strings are spaced closer together, they play as if they were at a higher tension. Once again, you must play with racquets designed with these new stringing techniques before you decide which type and design of string pattern to buy. Because of different head shapes, racquet designs, racquet materials, string designs, and string materials, the optimal string tension will vary from racquet to racquet and from player to player.

Sweet Spots

There are actually *three* sweet spots on a racquet's face. Each sweet spot measures a different physical characteristic of your racquet. The sweet spot that most of us think of is the place on the strings where the ball rebounds with the most power, or, technically, the spot on the racquet with the maximum coefficient of restitution. The second sweet spot is where the least amount of initial shock is given to your hand and arm. This is known as the center of percussion. The third sweet spot is the node or the place where the least amount of vibration occurs after the initial ball impact. Normally all three sweet spots do not occur in the same location. Usually the node is located near the center of the racquet with the center of percussion and maximum coefficient of restitution below center in that order. These three sweet spot locations are affected by your racquet's weight distribution, head size, flex, and shape. When manufacturers tell you that they have elongated or enlarged the sweet spot, they do not tell you which sweet spot or spots have changed. Hitting with a racquet is the only way to determine which sweet spot sizes and locations are right for you.

BALLS

Pressurized and nonpressurized balls, vividly colored and multicolored balls, and balls of different textures have all appeared on the market, but manufacturers have settled on a blue, nonpressurized ball. The professional International Racquetball Tour (I.R.T.) now uses a special green ball made by Penn. A nonpressurized ball obtains its bounce from the rubber from which it is made, rather than from air pressure within its hollow core. So, when you open a can of racquetballs, you will not hear the hissing sound you hear when opening a can of tennis balls.

Racquetballs must meet official standards of size, bounce, and weight, and these standards should be indicated on the package. Although many lesser known racquetball brands still circulate on the market, Penn, Ektelon, Kennex, and Wilson are the leading manufacturers. All of these manufacturers produce quality products, but Penn and Ektelon racquetballs are the standard of the industry and are used most in tournaments. Balls usually sell for $2.50 to $5.00 for a can of two.

GLOVES

If you are going to play serious racquetball, you need a glove. You have a choice between partial-finger and full-finger racquetball gloves. Some players prefer to create their own partial-finger gloves by cutting the fingers out of full-fingered gloves so they can grip better and can get a better feel on their grip. Others prefer full-finger gloves because the purpose of the glove is to keep the hand dry and to prevent blisters. They feel partial-finger gloves do not afford the dryness or protection of a full glove. Select a glove type according to your individual taste.

Another consideration in glove selection is the material from which the glove is made. Deerskin gloves are the most popular leather gloves, but a few companies are making gloves with other leathers such as goatskin and pigskin. The only challenge to deerskin is coming from synthetic materials. A synthetic suede leather that is soft, does not stiffen as readily from salts, and can be washed is now on the market.

Wash the glove by hand using a mild soap and lukewarm water. Rinse your glove thoroughly and allow it to dry flat on a towel or similar absorbing surface. Sometimes it is helpful to slip on the glove to form it to your hand before it totally dries. Remember that after you wash your glove, it will never feel the same or be as soft as when it was new, but it will usually be better than it was before washing.

When you buy a glove, choose one that forms to your hand and fingers. It should be neither too tight nor too loose. The glove should have tucked inseams for comfort, and all seams should be reinforced in the stress areas at the finger base and the back of the hand closure. Almost all gloves have large Velcro closures, and these are excellent. Another important feature is the amount of ventilation the glove affords your hand. Look at the back and the fingers of the glove to determine if holes or mesh is provided for air to get to your skin. If you are a diver, you will like a padded glove.

You have a choice of colors and manufacturers from which to pick. A few of the better known racquetball glove companies are Penn, Champion, Trophy, SAI, Saranac, and Ektelon. The price range of a glove varies from around $10 to about $16. Take some time in the selection process. If you can borrow and try different types of gloves from friends, do so.

SHOES

The racquetball shoe is specially designed for quick starts and rapid changes of motion. In order to serve this purpose, the shoe must have gum rubber soles (see Figure 1.4) and reinforced uppers to withstand great forces. Note that the gum rubber is continuous onto part of the upper. This is important since in racquetball you push off on the sides of your feet, and the wraparound gum rubber gives you the needed traction. Shoes should also be lightweight and have well-built insoles and midsoles. The uppers may be nylon, nylon mesh, synthetic leather, or leather. The leading manufacturers of racquetball shoes are Adidas, Brooks, Converse, Reebok, Foot-Joy, Kaepa, Ektelon, Nike, and Head. The price range of racquetball shoes is usually

Figure 1.4   Look for racquetball shoes with wraparound gum rubber soles that give you good traction when you push off with the sides of your feet.

between $40 and $120. You can purchase racquetball shoes in club shops, sport-specific footwear shops, and large sporting goods stores.

Get the right fit. Of course, as a potential shoe buyer you cannot test the shoe by playing racquetball in it; however, you can wear your sweat socks to the shoe store to give you a truer sense of fit. You can also run, stop, push off, and change directions rapidly to assess the shoe in the store. Most racquetball shoes maintain their size and will not stretch after you play in them, so "if the shoe fits, wear it" is a good policy. All racquetball shoes are durable on wood floors, but if worn on a rough surface, such as macadam, the sole will quickly wear out.

It is a good idea to walk (inside) in your new shoes for a few days before playing in them. When you do go to the court, it would be helpful to take your old shoes and some adhesive bandages in case you get hot spots and blisters. Even with quality new shoes, the stress from racquetball's sudden and quick movements can cause foot problems. It might be a good idea to play in new shoes for one game and then switch to your old shoes as a preventive measure. If the insole of your shoe deteriorates faster than the rest of your shoe, you may replace all or part of the insole with sorbothane replacements.

Do not wear other sport-specific shoes when playing racquetball. A running shoe, tennis shoe, or other sport-specific shoe is designed for its own sport, not racquetball.

EYE GUARDS

Wear eye guards. Most clubs provide them on request, and most clubs require them. Many types of eye guards are on the market, but they can be divided into two basic groups: nonhinged plastic guards and hinged plastic guards. Nonhinged guards are attached to your head with an elastic band. There are no moveable parts to break on these guards. The nonhinged guard is usually shaped to your face contour so there is little room for air circulation and there is constant fogging on the lenses.

Hinged guards have moveable parts so they tend to break. They are made like regular glasses with an attached elastic band to keep them securely on your head. Hinged guards do not fog as much as nonhinged guards since air can easily circulate around the lenses.

All guards afford excellent protection for the eyes. The problem with all guards is that the lenses get dirty and scratched, and perspiration forms more readily around the eyes, which causes visual acuity problems. Most new closed-lens eye protection is fog and scratch resistant. They will, however, after some use, scratch and fog. Most eye guards range in price from $8 to $35. However, cost should be of little concern for preservation of eyesight. An eye injury can be devastating, and prevention is worth everything.

EQUIPMENT BAGS

Many players use a carrying bag for clothes, racquets, and other gear. A few major characteristics to look for in a carrying bag are size, shape, number of compartments, and quality of construction. Obtain a bag large enough for all the items you are likely to carry; think in terms of seasonal changes and warm-ups (see Figure 1.5). Consider how the bag's compartments will allow you to organize your gear, keep wet items away from other items (in a separate waterproof area), and house your racquet. All carrying bags should have rein-

Figure 1.5 Pick a racquetball carrying bag large enough for you to organize all your gear.

forced construction around the seams and the handle-area stress points. Other points to consider are color, ventilation, type of handle or straps for carrying, and closures.

SELECTING A RACQUETBALL FACILITY

Choose a racquetball facility after visiting a few and asking a lot of questions. Talk to employees and members to find out what they have to say. If you know someone who is a member, talk with him or her before you visit.

From this point on your selection should be based on your individual needs and wants. Some of the major considerations for selecting a facility pertain solely to racquetball. These include cost, courts, waiting time, tournaments, and instructor-pro availability.

Key Elements for Selecting Racquetball Equipment

- A smaller grip size allows for more wrist action and power than a larger grip size, which stabilizes the wrist and forearm more.

- Hitting with a variety of racquets and grip sizes is the best method of determining the correct racquet and grip size.

- A racquet with flat sides and top makes it easier to play balls hugging the wall and floor.

- Buy brand-name racquetball products.

- Lightweight racquets are more advantageous for the control player and heavyweight racquets are more advantageous for the power player.

- Be aware and cautious when purchasing any new product on the racquetball market.

- Use lower string tension for more power and tighter strings for more control.

- Eye injuries are a risk in racquetball. Wear eye guards!

- Wear a glove to prevent blisters and to keep perspiration off your racquet hand.

- Wear sport-specific racquetball shoes that enhance your movement skills and prevent injuries.

You may also keep in mind some nonracquetball-related factors. Remember, a club can serve as a place to relax, get fit, and meet others as well as a place to perfect your kill shots. Use the tips that follow and the Facility Selection Checklist on pages 20-21 to help you pick the club that's right for you.

Cost

Cost concerns include the initial membership fee as well as the dues and court costs associated with the club. The cost for membership varies. Initiation fees can run from $100 to over $1,000, and yearly fees might be in the $300 to $600 range. Court-time fees might range from $2 an hour per person to $10 an hour per person. Court fees also vary with time of day and day of week, so you need to have an idea of when you will be playing most of your matches. Also consider other cost items such as instructor-pro fees; guest fees; service fees for towels, hair dryers, and locker rental; tournament entry fees; parking fees; and discount-cost factors for family and group memberships.

Type of Courts

Courts play differently depending on the materials from which their walls are constructed. Determine whether you prefer to play on panel walls, cement or block walls, or glass walls, and find a facility that meets your needs. Check out the courts. Eyeball the panels to make sure they are not bowed. Look for small holes or cracks in cement walls. Also, make sure lights, door jambs, air vents, and other fixtures are flush with the ceilings and walls. You don't need to learn how to play crazy caroms from cracked walls and poorly constructed courts.

Floor surface is also important, and usually you will have to choose between a wood and synthetic floor. Wood floors seem to be much more amenable to racquetball movement patterns than synthetic floors because you can slide much more easily on wood.

Consider court lighting—including total illumination of the court, spot brightness problems, glare problems, and light color—when making your facility choice. Checking total illumination involves being sure that there is ample lighting in the court as well as equal lighting in both the front and the back sections of the court. If the court is not well lighted or is not consistently lighted throughout, you will have trouble visually following the racquetball as it moves through the court. Glare, or excessive brightness, on the floor or walls can interfere with your watching and following the ball. Light colors vary with the type of lighting system used. Fluorescents give a white light; incandescents, an off-white light; metal halides, a bluish to pinkish light; and sodium lights, a yellowish light. If your home court has a distinct hue, you may have difficulty adjusting to courts with other lighting systems when you play tournaments.

Court ventilation is important. If ventilation is not adequate, moisture forms on the walls and the courts become unplayable. Proper ventilation keeps the court cool so that perspiration is minimized. This prevents the development of wet spots on the floor that might be slippery and create inconsistent bounces.

A last item to consider is the availability of equipment storage both inside and outside the court for your warm-up clothing, extra racquets, and valuables. With the cost of equipment and clothing today, you can't afford to lose racquets or warm-ups because of insufficient court storage areas. A small flush wall box inside the court allows room for wallets, jewelry, and extra balls.

Time

With today's fast pace and limited time for lunch and exercise breaks, quick court occupancy is paramount. Consider how far in advance you must reserve court time and how long you are allowed to play at a given time. For example, if you have an hour to play at lunch time, can you be assured of a full hour's play or must you wait 10 or 15 minutes before you can start? Will you have to quit in the middle of a tight game to allow the next waiting players to move onto the court? These questions should be answered to your satisfaction before you commit to a racquetball facility.

Tournaments

The tournament offerings of a facility are certainly a consideration in the selection process. Does the facility host regular tournaments, and does it sponsor state, regional, and national tournaments? Does the facility provide tournaments for all players—for novice or C-level to open divisions? Are there tournaments for men, women, seniors, masters, and children? Are there doubles and mixed doubles tournaments, and does the facility provide challenge courts for members? If so, when?

Your interest in tournaments might be important in your facility selection. For the tournament-oriented player, a higher membership cost may be offset by the availability of many tournaments. For beginners who would not take advantage of the tournaments, the membership and court fees may become prohibitive.

Professional Instruction

The last major area of concern in facility selection might be the availability of a teaching pro. Is there a pro? Is the instruction good?

Is the pro's background strong? Are teaching aids such as ball machines, videotape units, and computer analysis available? Is there an extra cost for lessons, and, if so, what are the prices? Do touring pros make stops at this facility? Do they play in open tournaments, pro stops, or give clinics? Is there a pro shop where you can obtain needed instructional items and basic racquetball items? These are important questions if you are looking for a facility at which you would like to take formal instruction.

THE FACILITY SELECTION CHECKLIST

Use the form on the following pages to check those items that are important to you as a prospective facility member. First decide if you are looking at facilities specifically for racquetball or if you are also looking for other facility activities and offerings.

Facility Selection Checklist

Club address _____   Date of visit _____
           _____   Contact person _____
           _____
Phone   _____

1. Courts
   number   _____
   condition   _____
   type   _____
   lighting   _____
   ventilation   _____

2. Cost
   initiation   _____
   membership dues   _____
   court fees   _____
   guest fees   _____
   instructional fees _____

3. Instruction
   pro available   _____
   competence   _____
   background   _____
   touring pro clinics _____

4. Pro shop
   hours of operation   _____
   equipment rentals available _____

5. On-site tournaments
   frequency   _____
   ability levels _____
   entry fees   _____

6. Other fitness equipment
   ___ free weights   ___ hydrostatic weighing tank
   ___ machine weights   ___ pool
   ___ track   ___ treadmill
   ___ stationary bikes   ___ others: _____
                             _____

7. **Other fitness activities**

___ aerobics   ___ handball   ___ Jazzercise

___ self-defense   ___ squash   ___ tennis

___ wallyball   ___ weight lifting   ___ yoga

___ others: _____

8. **Relaxation and social amenities**

___ family activities   ___ juice/healthfood bar

___ large screen TV   ___ music

___ restaurant   ___ sauna

___ singles activities   ___ steam room

___ suntan booth   ___ wet bar

___ whirlpool   ___ others: _____

_____

9. **Family orientation**

child care facilities _____

fitness programs for kids _____

10. **General conditions**

parking _____

locker room facilities and amenities _____

cleanliness _____

adequate size of areas that I will use _____

number of units (racquetball courts, weight machines, etc.) _____

_____

11. **Other specific needs (list below)**

Chapter 2

Conditioning and Safety

*I*njuries are inevitable for a serious racquetball player, but you can work to keep them at a minimum. The keys are conditioning and safety. Racquetball is a power game and generating this power takes its toll on your body. If you are grooming for tournament play, coping with physical stress is crucial because of the number of matches that you will play in a short time. Is your body ready to give what it takes to win? If you're not fully physically fit for play, you're risking injury. Thus conditioning—and a little common sense—is the way to better, healthier racquetball.

CONDITIONING

Conditioning for racquetball, like any other sport, serves two functions. First, conditioning is a great way to prevent injuries, and second, conditioning properly done can improve your skill level. The best conditioning programs for athletes are tailored to meet the demands of their sport. The exercise programs we'll discuss in this chapter are those that are specific to the skills and demands of the game.

Racquetball takes a great deal of energy and some degree of cardiorespiratory endurance. The skills that are used are varied yet repetitive; therefore, specific muscular endurance is needed. The major body parts involved in racquetball are the legs for bending, stretching, stopping, and starting; the arm, especially the forearm, for wrist action; the torso for basic power; and the shoulder for arm action in the backswing, swing, and follow-through. Those are the basic, specific body parts to think about in conditioning for racquetball. However, remember that many other areas of the body come into play in racquetball as in any other sport. Cardiorespiratory conditioning, flexibility, muscular endurance, skills training, and a strength and power program are all necessary to improve your game.

Cardiorespiratory Conditioning

Since racquetball demands long-term endurance and short bursts of power, you should condition for these specifics. You may jump rope, run, swim, ride a bicycle, or run steps nonstop for 30 to 45 minutes to build up long-term cardiorespiratory fitness. Begin with short workouts of around 5 minutes, and over time, build up to 40 minutes or more with nonstop activity. You should do cardiorespiratory conditioning three or four days per week.

For short bursts of energy you can run sprints, run steps, swim sprints, or jump rope alternating between a fast and slow tempo. Use the same approach in bicycling; sprint in bursts and then ride at a normal speed. In all sprint training, as in other cardiorespiratory training, you need to start on a small scale and work toward a goal of 30 to 40 minutes. You may also play racquetball nonstop for about 40 minutes using maximum output on every shot to help with cardiorespiratory conditioning.

Most facilities now have computerized weight machines. For cardiorespiratory training using the lower body, stationary bicycles, stair climbers, and the versa climber work well. For upper body training, the rowing machine and the versa climber are effective. If you use these machines, you must start out for a short time, about 5 minutes, and work your way up to around 30 to 40 minutes. If you have not worked out before or have not completed this type of workout for some time, you should consult a physician first before beginning your training.

Flexibility

You can attain or maintain flexibility by static stretching, that is, by stretching and holding the stretch position. Do not bounce when you stretch. You should combine in your program leg stretching, lower back stretching, torso stretching, and arm-shoulder stretching. In static stretching (a stretch that you hold as illustrated in Figure 2.1) you need to fully stretch your muscles and hold the full stretch for 25 to 30 seconds.

Figure 2.1 A typical static stretch: stretch your muscles and *hold* the stretch for 25-30 seconds.

Playing racquetball and lifting free weights or using machine weights also aid in stretching. This stretching is dynamic in nature and you must use the full range of motion of any muscle group you are stretching. Ballet, modern dance, and some of the Far Eastern art forms like Tai-Chi are also great ways to stretch. In stretching, as in all conditioning, start slowly and build from there.

Muscular Endurance

Muscular endurance is the ability of a certain muscle or group of muscles to perform a movement over and over without that movement disintegrating. You can develop muscular endurance specifically for racquetball in two ways. First, practice racquetball skills. You can hit 300 ceiling shots, 300 kills, 100 Z serves, and so forth. Use both forehands and backhands because each technique uses slightly different muscle groups. Hit the skills in succession, for at least 35 to 45 minutes. Not only are you conditioning, you are also grooving your strokes (see our upcoming discussion of skills training). Second, you can weight train. When lifting weights for endurance you should do three to five sets of 12 to 15 repetitions each. Later in this chapter we will give you some racquetball-specific weight training exercises. To gain muscular endurance, it is more effective to do high repetitions with a lighter weight than to do low repetitions with a high weight.

Skills Training

You can improve your racquetball skills by practicing each skill either in strict practice sessions or in game situations. It becomes very easy only to play practice games and never, or rarely, to practice just the skills. You need to do both. Both are specific, and you cannot attain total skill conditioning without doing both.

When skills training consists of playing games, it is important to play against many different opponents. If you always play the same opponent, you will learn only how to play against this opponent. Your skill acquisition will be minimal. However, if you play many different people, you maximize your skills acquisition. It is also important to play against people who are better than you. You learn much more.

Try to skill train five days per week. Practice skills for 45 minutes to one hour, three days per week. Go into the court by yourself or with a partner and have a skills schedule to follow. Work on a specific skill from a particular portion of the court, and perform it over and over. During this hour hit somewhere around 400 to 500 balls.

If you have a friend who plays at a higher skill level than you, ask her or him to help with your skill learning. Obtain instruction from the racquetball pro if your facility has one. Lastly, arrange to be videotaped practicing and playing games and then review the tape with a more skilled player. Later in this book we provide a shot analysis chart that will help with skills building.

Strength and Power

The last aspect of racquetball-specific conditioning is strength and power, a major concern for all players. The best way to increase strength and power is to offer resistance to your muscles over a distance or through a range of motion. This is the basic "overload" principle, and weight training can best complete this portion of your conditioning program. You can use free weights, dumbbells or barbells, or machine weights. Again, as in all conditioning programs, start with very light weights and work up. If you have not seriously lifted weights before, get training from a knowledgeable training specialist who will be able to coach you in the proper technique for resistance training.

Let's look first at the legs. Squats are excellent for the legs. Do them at an even pace and do not bounce when you are fully squatted. Leg extensions and leg flexions on a leg machine work both your upper and lower legs. The leg press on a weight machine is similar to the squat exercise and gives a good workout to the upper front of the leg. Toe raises build the calf area of the lower leg. A leg extension machine and the hamstring machine also provide good leg strength conditioning.

Next, let's look at some shoulder weight-training activities. Any type of press, including the military and bench press, is excellent for shoulder development. Pull-ups and dips, on a pull-up bar or parallel bars, are also good for shoulders. Biceps curls put significant stress on the shoulders, so you should include them in your conditioning program. Lateral pull-downs also significantly work on the shoulder area.

An important part of weight-training is developing your forearms. The forearms control the wrist and finger actions. Strong wrists and fingers are necessary for playing racquetball well. The hitting wrist action involves all three major muscle groups in the forearm: the flexor muscles on the inside of your forearm, the extensor muscles on the back of your forearm, and the rotator muscles on both sides of your forearm. A weight-conditioning program for the forearms must develop each of these three muscle groups.

Use dumbbells or barbells for prone and supine wrist curls. The supine wrist curl shown in Figure 2.2 works on the forehand wrist snap and the stabilization of your racquet on all forehand shots.

The prone wrist curl shown in Figure 2.3 develops the extensor muscles on the back of the forearm. These muscle groups are important for backhand wrist snap and stabilization of your racquet in all backhand shots.

The wrist snap of racquetball not only moves back and forth but also turns. The last group of forearm muscles are the deep muscles—the wrist rotators. Wrist rotation muscles can be strengthened by using dumbbells in the supine position and rotating the dumbbell inward and back to the starting position (see Figure 2.4).

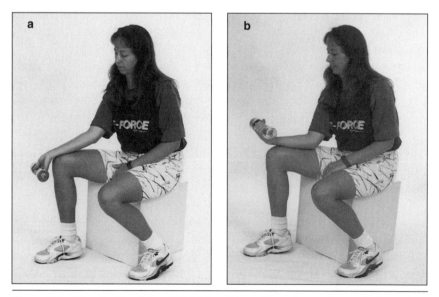

Figure 2.2 The starting (a) and finishing (b) positions for supine curls for wrist flexor development. This exercise may be performed with barbells or dumbbells.

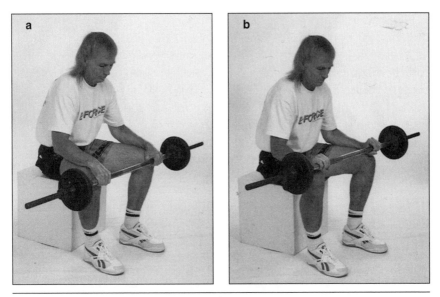

Figure 2.3 The starting (a) and finishing (b) positions for prone curls for wrist extensor development. This exercise may be performed with barbells or dumbbells.

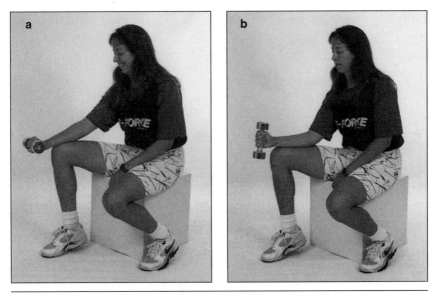

Figure 2.4 Wrist rotation dumbbell curls encourage forearm rotator development. Rotate from the starting position (a) to the ending position (b).

Biceps curls significantly stress the forearm, so they serve a dual purpose for both shoulder and arm conditioning.

A standing prone wrist roller exercise works well to build the rotator muscles in the forearm. Figure 2.5 shows the grip on a small piece of round wood to which is tied a rope. At the bottom of the rope is a weight. You turn the wood bar in your hands to lift the weight to it. After you have lifted the weight, lower it in the same fashion. This exercise is also effective for increasing finger strength. Again, wrist rotation is important for all power shots in the game.

Figure 2.5   Roll a rope for forearm development.

Another exercise for developing finger, arm, shoulder, and upper back strength is a fingertip push-up. You can do fingertip push-ups on the floor with the body horizontal or standing against a wall (see Figure 2.6).

Distribute the weight of your body between your fingers and feet. Keeping your body straight, bend your elbows until your chin touches either the floor or the wall. Wall fingertip push-ups are easier to do because most of your weight is supported by your feet. Finally, a simple exercise for finger strength and forearm flexors is just to squeeze a racquetball.

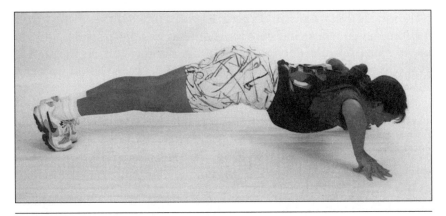

Figure 2.6 Try fingertip push-ups on the floor or against the wall for finger and forearm development.

Here are some conditioning tips that can help prevent problems with your lower back and ankles. For the lower back, lie flat on your back with arms on the floor, palms down, and feet flat on the floor with the knees bent. Reach and grasp one knee at a time and pull the knee toward the chest. The knee always stays bent. After doing the same with the other knee, you can pull both knees simultaneously to the chest. Remember, knees stay bent throughout this exercise. You can strengthen your ankles by doing toe and heel raises with your body weight or with additional weights. Stand erect, roll up to your toes, hold, and then do the same onto your heels. You can also rotate your feet in, out, up, and down and hold. You can do this exercise sitting or standing; however, the standing position puts more stress on your ankles. You can do these exercises with foot weights when sitting or on a seated or standing calf-raise machine. Standard sit-ups or crunches can also help alleviate back pain and strengthen upper body rotation.

Weight training for strength should consist of three sets of five repetitions each. These routines are done with a weight that permits you to barely complete the three sets of five.

A new weight-training concept called "periodization" has recently proved to be an effective strength-gaining regimen. It is set up with three weeks of doing three sets of five repetitions each, three weeks of five sets of ten repetitions each, and one week of three sets of two repetitions each. In each period, maximum weight is employed so that you can just barely complete the routine. With periodization, after the seven weeks of training, you take a week off and then you begin all over. One desirable aspect of periodization technique is that it can build you to a peak. For example, if you begin training seven weeks before a tournament, you peak for the tournament. The program encompasses both strength and endurance. If you'd like to try periodization techniques, consult a training professional.

Diet and psychological conditioning are also important dimensions of a racquetball conditioning program. Your diet should be well-rounded with the proper intake of vitamins, minerals, carbohydrates, fats, and proteins. With a well-balanced diet, the typical racquetball player doesn't need to take supplements. When you play at the highest skill levels and are constantly training, six to eight hours a day, pushing your body to its maximum levels, supplements are very useful.

Psychological conditioning can't be overlooked. You need to have a positive mental set. First, racquetball is something you should look forward to. Second, you will play better with positive mental imagery. You will enjoy your sport whether you win or lose, whether you are practicing or playing. Think positive. Later in chapter 15 we will provide in-depth conditioning programs, diet regime, and discuss the use of sport psychology specialists for taking your game to its highest level.

If you're serious about your racquetball, you owe it to yourself to incorporate the preceding exercises into a carefully thought-out training regimen. You may start with the sample conditioning schedule presented here and build from it.

SAFETY

Some racquetball injuries, such as blisters, sprains, and soreness, can result from the natural course of play. Others are incidental. These arise from carelessness. Let's look at ways of preventing both kinds of injuries.

Incidents, Accidents, and Injuries

Incidents and accidents are caused by (albeit sometimes minor) character flaws—not by the physical demands of the sport. These injuries are easy to prevent if you follow three simple guidelines:

Sample Conditioning Schedule	
Monday	Play racquetball (60 minutes) Run, swim, or bicycle (30 minutes) Static stretch (20-30 minutes)
Tuesday	Lift weights (60-90 minutes) Include: squats, leg extensions, ankle work, biceps curls, military press, bench press, pull-ups, dips, sit-ups on incline bench (bent knee), and wrist work (flexing, extending, and rotating) Practice racquetball skills (45-60 minutes)
Wednesday	Play racquetball (60 minutes) Run, swim, or bicycle (30 minutes) Static stretch (20-30 minutes)
Thursday	Lift weights (60-90 minutes) Include: squats, leg extensions, ankle work, biceps curls, military press, bench press, pull-ups, dips, sit-ups on incline bench (bent knee), and wrist work (flexing, extending, and rotating) Practice racquetball skills (45-60 minutes)
Friday	Play racquetball (60 minutes) Run, swim, or bicycle (30 minutes) Static stretch (20-30 minutes)
Saturday	Lift weights (60-90 minutes) Include: squats, leg extensions, ankle work, biceps curls, military press, bench press, pull-ups, dips, sit-ups on incline bench (bent knee), and wrist work (flexing, extending, and rotating) Practice racquetball skills (45-60 minutes)
Sunday	Off (rest)

1. **Don't be a jerk and don't tolerate jerks.** Many accidents occur after the point is won or lost when a player, out of frustration, slams a dead ball or bangs a racquet into the wall. When the point is through, your opponent shouldn't need to be concerned about dangerous objects flying around the court. Keep a lid on your emotions and insist that your opponents do the same.

2. **Know where you are.** Scoring points isn't worth hitting some-one with your racquet. When you know your opponent is nearby,

either let up on your swing, or stop, call a hinder, and replay the point. Ask your opponent to do the same. Remember also that walls, like a rude opponent, won't get out of your way. When your back is literally up against the wall, adjust your swing to more of a scraping action. A full-blown backswing will cause your racquet to impact the wall and your elbow will pay the price. Try to keep an arm's length away from side walls and corners.

3. **Use your equipment properly.** If your eyes are important to you, wear some type of eye guard whenever you step into the court. Don't wear your glasses in place of eye guards. Eyeglasses are weakly hinged and are probably not made of polycarbonate, the strong plastic from which most eye guards are constructed. Always attach the racquet thong to your wrist so the racquet will not fly free and hit you or your opponent. Finally, wear shoes that fit properly and take good care of your glove. Blister the ball—not your feet and hands.

Warm Up to Injury Prevention

Warming up is an interesting phenomenon. Warm-ups can aid performance or prevent injuries or both. The research on the benefits of warming up to improve performance is inconclusive. Some investigations have shown that warming up enhances performance; other studies have shown no difference in performance with or without warm-ups. We do know that warming up stretches and warms the muscles because of an increase in blood flow. This warming can help prevent muscle strain and certain injuries.

The most effective warm-up is specific to each player, so the types of warm-up vary. Some players, for example, hit a variety of shots easily and then hit them progressively harder. Others stretch, do calisthenics, run in place, or run around the court. Still others do many different types of warm-ups.

Warm-ups may have psychological as well as physiological benefits. If a player *thinks* the warm-up is helping to improve skill performance, then it may actually improve performance. In any case, warm up at your pace. Do what feels good for you. Think about the forearms, shoulders, lower back, and legs as the prime movers in the skills of racquetball and make sure your warm-up routines stretch these areas before you begin a strenuous workout or match.

Alleviating Common Ailments

If you play the game for any length of time, you're bound to suffer an injury now and then. Adequate conditioning, warming up, and playing it safe can't prevent all your aches and pains. The table below details the treatment and cause of some of the most common ailments you're likely to face.

Alleviating Common Ailments		
Ailment	**Possible Causes**	**Remedy or Prevention Strategies**
Ankle problems	Weak ankles	Ankle-specific conditioning
	Improper shoes	Taping from an expert—do not substitute an Ace bandage ankle wrap for athletic tape
		High top shoes if you need more support
Feet blisters	Poor fitting shoes	Wear proper shoes
	Wetness	Wear two pairs of socks (not tube socks)
	Friction during stops and starts	Use foot powder
		Use donut pad
		Use petroleum jelly to combat friction
Hand blisters	Racquet twists on contact with ball	Use glove, Band-Aids, athletic tape, or donut pad
		Check grip and handle for correct size and condition
Sore elbows	Faulty technique	Be sure your arm is bent slightly when your racquet contacts the ball; your arm should not be rigid
	Racquet vibration	Try a more flexible racquet
	Overuse	Ice elbow before and after playing
		Rest
Lower back soreness	Player not used to bending and staying low	Perform stretches specifically for lower back conditioning such as back hyperextensions, straight leg crossovers, and trunk twists

Key Elements for Safety and Conditioning

- Wear eye guards at all times when playing racquetball.
- Don't swing when your opponent is in your way.
- Keep the court floor dry.
- Wear proper shoes and socks.
- Employ warm-ups that meet your own personal needs.
- Use conditioning exercises to prevent injuries and to increase your racquetball skills.
- Include cardiorespiratory conditioning, flexibility, muscular endurance, skills routines, and strength and power in your training program.
- Individualize your program to meet your needs, desires and level of skill that you wish to reach.

Chapter 3

Determining Your Playing Level

Photo by Charlie Palek—KILLSHOT magazine

*T*here is a wide range of abilities among racquetball players. Playing level is a composite of many factors—knowledge of strategy, ability to hit with power and accuracy, patience, and so on—that will be discussed in this chapter.

Knowing your current level of play is helpful in setting goals. It may also be useful in placing yourself at the proper level in club tournaments. However, the most important concept to learn is that you can change your level of play by using the ideas in this book. Let's start out by determining your level of play.

WHAT'S YOUR ABILITY LEVEL?

Playing levels begin at the novice or beginning level and end at the highest level of play, the touring pro. It is important to find your level of play to determine what skills you need to take your game to the next level.

Novice Player

The novice is a beginner, and a wide range of skills can be found among players in this class. The novice has little court sense regarding deflection and rebound action of the ball, especially out of the corners. He or she may not understand the importance of center-court positioning, and usually does not knowingly attempt to hold center court. The beginning player has some knowledge of the rules of racquetball but little insight into the strategies of the game. As a result, many balls are played high, and the player does not consistently bend at the knees. In addition, the novice player lacks the patience to wait on the ball; as a result, overhand shots are prevalent. Being unaware of how to stroke the ball with full power, a beginner usually hits shots with slow to intermediate speed. A novice tends to follow the ball with the body rather than with the eyes, and seems to spend much time chasing around the court, as seen in Figure 3.1.

C-Player

The C-player is an advanced novice who has some knowledge of the passing shot, the kill shot, and a few serves. He or she uses strategy on occasion but is seldom consistent in using strategy. The C-player kills inconsistently, hits fairly good passing shots, is beginning to perfect one good serve, and follows the ball with his or her body, but not as often as the novice. Some low shots, as a result of bending the knees properly, are evident. The C-player understands strategy and the importance of center-court positioning but still lacks patience

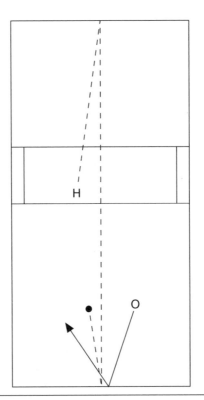

Figure 3.1 A novice player does not anticipate where the ball will bounce and literally chases the ball around the court.

and too often plays the ball high. The C-player is beginning to understand rebounding and angles in the court; in addition, he or she is learning to hit the ball hard but seldom with control. The C-player can employ ceiling shots with some effectiveness, and the high-level C-player can kill the ball fairly well on the forehand shot when positioned in center court or frontcourt.

B-Player

He or she is beginning to look like a racquetball player. The B-player consistently uses a lethal kill shot on the forehand, uses the passing shot effectively, and plays the ceiling shot well, especially on defense. The B-player understands strategy and uses it about 75 percent of the time, but correct use of strategy remains inconsistent.

Although the importance of center court is understood, and the B-player attempts to maintain center-court position, he or she relinquishes it often. The B-player understands and reacts to most angles and rebounds. The backhand is consistent but only occasionally used as an offensive weapon. The B-player more consistently keeps the ball lower than the C-player but still hits some high shots by mistake. The B-player possesses one excellent serve and two or three other less effective serves. The B-player is developing patience, hits many shots with power, and is consistent with more than half of them. The B-player lets most of the high balls go by and will play them off the back wall.

A-Player

When you reach the A-division, you are talking about the well-rounded player. The A-player may lack total consistency and may not be able to use all the minor shots in his or her game as part of an effective offense. The A-player is very patient, keeps the ball low, and has a lethal kill shot on both forehand and backhand strokes. In addition, passing shots are effective from all areas of the court and are a consistent part of the offensive game. The A-player effectively uses ceiling shots for both offense and defense. Strategy is used effectively most of the time, and short mental lapses occur rarely. Center-court position is constantly strived for and maintained whenever possible. The A-player hits the ball with power and authority on all strokes and possesses a wide variety of potent serves. The A-player demonstrates mastery of all basic skills on all strokes. He or she also knows to anticipate where the ball will bounce, and runs directly to that spot instead of chasing the ball from wall to wall (see Figure 3.2).

Open-Player

The open-player is the advanced A-player and displays all the skills one could ask for in racquetball. All shots can be used for offense, the ball is always hit crisply, and center-court position is maintained. Backhands and forehands are equally excellent. The open-player uses strategy continuously and effectively. The open-player is fluid, consistent, and practically error free. To win points against the open-

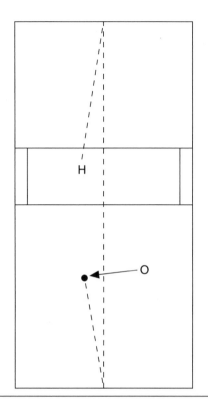

Figure 3.2 An A-player follows the ball's flight path with the eyes in order to anticipate where to meet the ball.

player, an opponent needs to hit with perfect placement; otherwise, the ball is returned.

Pro-Player

The pro-player is an open-player who possesses the maximum in consistency, experience, hitting power, and precision hitting skills. Touring pros are differentiated from open-players in that they can return almost all shots with offensive returns—unless the shot is a perfect placement. The anticipation and reaction of the touring pro are better than that of the open-player. Chapter 15 gives additional information on the training, activities, and life of a touring pro. Club pros generally have the touring pro's knowledge and understanding of the game although they may not play at the touring pro's level.

FACTORS INFLUENCING YOUR ABILITY AND OPPORTUNITY

There are numerous factors that may influence your ultimate racquetball achievement. Sex, age, experience, heredity, and dedication are the most important.

Sex

Like most new sports, racquetball was played predominantly by men at the outset, and women players were much less visible than their male counterparts. Women players are now making major inroads into the world of racquetball. The visibility of women's racquetball has been enhanced by the founding of the Women's Professional Racquetball Association (WPRA). More women's tournaments are being held than ever before, and divisions for women have been established in tournaments that were previously all male.

In many tournaments with women's and men's divisions, the women, like the men, are subdivided according to level of skill. Because there are fewer women players competing in tournaments than men, there are fewer subdivisions for women. We hope this will change soon and there will be similar subdivisions for men and women. In addition, many racquetball clubs are now catering to women players with women's in-house tournaments and challenge courts. Some clubs employ both a woman and a man as the club pros. The major difference between men and women players is that men normally hit the ball harder than women. Men are bigger and have more muscle mass than women, and this allows men to hit with more power. Other than power, women can perform all aspects of the game as well as men.

Age

Age is an important factor in designating racquetball skill level. Let's consider the special characteristics of very young players as well as the older racquetball enthusiast.

We are often asked when children should begin playing racquetball. Expose children to the racquetball court and racquetball game early—when they are between two and seven years of age. The important word is exposure. A child should see the court, the game, and the equipment and then be allowed to experiment on his or her own. If a child enjoys the racquetball environment, encourage him or her to continue to hit and play.

Racquetball should be like any other activity in the child's life at this point. The parents should not apply pressure to play racquetball or any other sport. If an activity is fun, children should pursue it at their pace. Remember that children from the ages of 2 to 12 years progress through various stages of physical development. These developmental stages will partially determine if a child is ready to handle the complexities of a physical skill like racquetball. You should also remember that these stages of physical development occur at different times in different children. A developmental stage necessary for learning certain skills in racquetball might occur at age 8 in one child, age 12 in another, and at age 6 in still another. Parents or instructors should not compare a child's skill level, ability, or interest with that of other children of the same age. Interest and skill proficiency are individual matters at this stage of the child's life.

Movement exploration can be very helpful for the young child. Also, exposure to a variety of types of balls, including large and small balls, soft and hard balls, and balls of various colors and textures, is intriguing to the young child. The same is true with racquets. You should provide smaller, lighter, plastic, colored, and other different kinds of racquets with which the child can experiment. At early ages, whether preschool or early school age, drilling on forehands, serves, and the backhand should not be done. Allow the child to bounce the ball high and low, to hit it soft, hard, low, high, and to hit the ball to different walls. Have the child stand facing forward, sideways, and backwards when trying to hit the ball. Let the child hit the ball after it bounces or experiment with playing the ball in the air before it bounces. Encourage questions and attempt to answer them on their level. Once the child shows interest, you can use simple activities such as relays, tag racquetball with yarn balls, multi-bounce racquetball, and many other fun games. Self-tests such as "How many times can you hit the ball in a minute?" or "How many times can you hit the front wall with the ball in 30 seconds?" can be fun for young children. As the child continues to show interest in racquetball, add modified games or lead-up games to the progression of skills. Play one-wall or two-wall games, games with multiple bounces, and games with different balls. Remember that each child progresses at his or her pace, from exposure to exploration to low-organized skills to modified games.

When the child is ready for competition and asks to compete, introduce the competitive aspects of the game. Even at this stage, a child should not be pushed into hours of drills and practice sessions. Young players should play and progress at their level, not at the level the parent-instructor wishes them to play. The first competitive game you should teach to children is "no bounce." In this game the ball may bounce as many times as needed until it is returned successfully.

When you expose your children to racquetball, listen to and answer their questions and allow them to have fun with racquetball within safe limits. This will help them develop a healthy attitude toward the sport. Remember to let the young players progress at their pace and to provide appropriate instruction if the young player shows an interest in competition.

Now, who is the older player? It could be someone over 30, over 40, or over 60 years of age. Children have developmental stages of skill levels, and adults have developmental stages of aging. Older players cannot, therefore, be classified by age alone. However, one method of classifying older players is to compare the older "first-time" player with the player who is older but has been playing the game for many years.

The first recommendation for the older first-time player is to have a complete physical, including a stress test, before stepping onto the court. If the examination and stress test indicate that you are healthy, you may slowly begin the adventure into the world of racquetball.

Slow and *cautious* are the two cornerstones for the beginning older player. Good, long warm-ups and stretching increase blood flow to the muscles and stretch the muscle fibers. You must remember that as the aging process continues, circulation slows down, maximum heart rate decreases, and maximum oxygen uptake (probably one of the best indications of cardiorespiratory fitness) decreases. Arthritis is much more prevalent among older players and can create many painful joint problems. Therefore, increase your playing slowly and do not overindulge. You should also be aware of the injury factor involved in participating in a new activity. As you get older, the rapid, "youthful" recovery from injury does not take place. Therefore, do everything in your control to prevent injury and avoid the long recovery period. Conditioning, stretching, warming up, good diet, and knowledge of safety factors are excellent methods of preventing injuries.

For the over-35 racquetball player, the game includes a slower-paced format, more strategy, and better shot placement. Tournaments have divisions for the 35-and-over (seniors), the 45-and-over (masters), and the 55-and-over (golden) age levels as well as various five-year intervals in between. Remember some older players in their 40s can keep up with players in their 20s. Both men and women can continue to be physically active throughout their lifetimes if they adjust their activity to accommodate the aging process. A complete physical examination including blood profiles and a stress test is recommended every other year from 30 to 40 years of age and each year after the age of 40.

Special Needs Player

Racquetball is so versatile that young people, older people, healthy people, or people with special needs can play. Sometimes the rules may need to be slightly altered, perhaps by allowing two bounces, to accommodate the special need, yet racquetball remains a fun game.

The player with a permanent disability must modify his or her game, shots, and strategies based on the degree of limitation of their special needs. Before beginning to play racquetball, you should check with your physician and, working together, set limits on your style of play. Individuals with visual, auditory, and ambulatory special needs can and do play racquetball. People with special developmental needs, people with special mental needs, or people who are recovering from heart surgery can play racquetball if they adjust the game so that it falls within their capabilities.

The individual with a temporary disability can also play racquetball if the game is adjusted. It is possible that you may not play competitively with temporary special needs but you may practice in an attempt to stay active. During a supposedly sedentary period, you should receive permission from your physician to participate.

Experience

Your level of experience will help you decide what type of player you are. For example, tournament play or instruction can make major differences in your playing style. The quality of opposition you play will also have some effect on how well you play. The number of years that you have participated should help you to understand strategies, angles of ball bounce, and opponent weaknesses. Experience then begins to mesh with ability. The longer you play and the more variety you encounter, the greater your levels of skill and strategy become, and the better player you become.

Heredity and Dedication

Conditioning and practice will improve anyone's ability. Some people have a genetic advantage that enables them to get more out of each training hour than others. This is related to the ratio of slow-twitch to fast-twitch muscle fibers found in working muscles. Racquetball favors people who have a higher concentration of fast-twitch muscle fibers. If you sense Mother Nature has dealt you a bad hand in the muscle fiber game, just know that you'll have to train harder and play smarter.

Dedication is important for success in any activity and racquetball is no different. You must be able to spend many hours conditioning, practicing, reading, learning, and playing racquetball. The more time you spend in dedicating yourself to racquetball, the better you will become. See chapter 15 for the ultimate in dedication.

YOU CAN GET THERE FROM HERE

The categorization mentioned will help you identify your beginning skill level and the skills you will need to progress. Practice, dedication, being physically fit, and understanding strategies will better allow you to move to the next level. Try to play at least three days a week and always try to play those players better than yourself.

You are now ready to move ahead into the skills chapters that follow. In them you'll find advice that you will need to understand and develop to move your game to the next level.

Key Elements for Determining Your Level of Racquetball Play

- If you have special needs, play racquetball under the direction of your physician.
- Players with special needs should adapt and modify the game to meet their individual needs.
- Employing skill drills rather than playing in game situations is important for the player with a temporary disability.
- Allow children to progress in racquetball at their pace.
- Allow the child's competitive spirit to emerge on its own.
- Older players should have a complete physical examination and stress test before beginning to play racquetball.
- Beginning older players should play racquetball slowly and cautiously, especially at first, to avoid undue stress and injury.

Part II

MASTERING
SKILLS
AND STRATEGIES

Chapter 4

Practicing and Drilling

Photo by Charlie Palek—KILLSHOT magazine

You step into the court for a tournament match and from the very first serve, you can do no wrong. Not only are your bread-and-butter shots sharper than they've ever been, but shots you've never tried before—shots you may never even have imagined—easily spring from your racquet. You are in the zone. You are a natural.

You've dreamed about it, and we have too.

Well, wake up. There's nothing natural about becoming a natural. You can get in the zone—and maybe once or twice in competition you can successfully hit a shot you've never tried—but you can't just one day expect to be in the zone. You have to work your way into it. In racquetball, work means practice sessions full of drills. This chapter gives you tips for working smart.

DRILLS

One of the most important ways to practice is the use of drills. Two ideas are important in drill practice. One is that you work from simple drills to complex drills, and the other is that you benefit from repetition. The ancient Romans used to say "Repetition is the mother of learning." And it's true.

Because a beginner can keep a ball in play after only a few times on the court, many do not spend time practicing skills and using drills. Like any sport, racquetball requires practice in game situations and in skill drills, and both are important components to successful racquetball.

Go From Simple to Complex

You'll find drill sections at the end of most of the remaining chapters of this book. Use them. They are designed to help you perfect specific shots or skills or combinations of shots and skills.

For now, we would like to discuss how to make your practice sessions successful by progressing from simple to complex drills. When you follow a prescribed drill and want to make it more challenging (and fun), remember that there are elements you can manipulate in any drill. You can change your position on the court, increase the pace of the ball, aim for specific target areas, bring in specialized equipment, or increase the number of skills you use in combination (making a drill for one skill into a drill for a two-shot combination, for example).

To illustrate these ideas, let's look at a drill to practice forehand kills. The easiest place to hit forehand kills successfully is close to the front wall, so we start our drill in the service zone. Next, it is easier to hit a kill low to the front wall if we contact the ball near the floor, so we use a low ball. It is also easier to hit a stationary ball or a ball with only one direction of force. How can you hit a stationary ball for kill practice? Use a tee. A ten-inch tall paper cup will do. Hitting the ball off the cup keeps the drill simple. Staying in the service area also keeps it simple. The actual swing and hit should be partial speed, maybe half- or three-quarter speed, for control purposes. Once you have the basics down, you'll want to make this drill more difficult. You can drop the ball low; move farther from the front wall; and hit harder. You can make it more difficult by having the ball moving not only up but forwards or backwards as well. You can also make it more difficult by changing the speed, angle, and height of the ball before contact is made. Building your drills from the simple to the complex is like working from the basic foundation of a building (simple) to the total structure (complex) of the building. The most complex drill includes both you and the ball moving. This complex drill technique is as close to a game situation as you can come.

Repetition

Drills allow you to get maximum benefits from practicing over a given time because of their repetitive form. Also, repetition will help perfect your skills. The recurring patterns used in drills can help speed up the learning sequences in skill acquisition.

There is no magic number of how many times you should hit one drill or how often you should practice drills. But we generally recommend that you hit a minimum of 100 balls on a given drill. The number of times you practice this drill, say three or four times a week, will depend on how your skill is improving and how good you ultimately would like to be. You should know that the more you drill and the more you practice, the better you will become. Being a great racquetball player takes time and much drilling and practicing. See chapter 15 for Woody's intense practice and drilling schedule.

One of the problems is that practice drills can be boring because of their repetition. To avoid boredom, think creatively and modify your drills. For example, in the kill drill previously mentioned, you could attach targets, such as jar lids, paper, balloons, or cups, to the front wall, and you could raise and lower the tee. Adding some diversity to drills can spice up your practice sessions. For some players practicing and drilling to music makes the long hours easier to manage. Drilling is essential to successful racquetball playing, so take time each week to drill as well as play.

With all drills you should set prepractice goals and write down how you are going to achieve your goals. A prepractice goal would be to hit 100 crosscourt passing shots from deep in your backhand corner three days per week. Initially you would like to accomplish a success rate of 50%. When you are able to do this successfully on each of your three days of practice, move your goal higher to a 60% success rate. Set realistic goals that are attainable in a reasonable amount of time.

Individual practice sessions should last between one and two hours. You should hit enough repetitions to achieve a groove. When finished with your individual drills, assess your progress. You can also drill with a partner. One person hits a certain shot repeatedly and the other person returns the shot in the same fashion. Quality practice time of short duration is usually more worthwhile than long sessions of lower quality.

Key Elements for Drills

- Spend at least 70% of your practice time on drills.
- Drill from simple to complex.
- Practice *does* make perfect.

Taking Your Game to Its Highest Level *Woody Clouse*

The amount of time you spend working on your racquetball skills will dictate your degree of success. If you wish to become the best racquetball player you can, you will need to spend up to 10 hours per week on drills and 8 to 10 hours per week practice playing. When you practice play you are out not only to win, but also to employ your newly learned skills from drilling. Practice play is taking those drills and putting them into use in game situations. In each of the coming skills chapters, the drills section is preceded by a few statements called "Taking Your Game to Its Highest Level." This is the definitive information you'll need to be the most successful racquetball player possible. Take time to read this information, put it into practice, and achieve the zone.

- Drills reinforce the muscle memory needed to create the consistency to move to the next level.

- Drills should be done twice as much as game playing.

- Racquetball is a sport of angles and repetition. Practicing drills is the only way to obtain the consistency needed at the highest levels.

- Your body needs to know how to perform all the shots in the game without involving a thought process.

Chapter 5

Hitting Forehand and Backhand Shots

Photo by Charlie Palek—KILLSHOT magazine

*T*he two primary racquetball shots are the forehand, hitting from the side of your dominant hand, and the backhand, hitting from the side of your nondominant hand. Although these strokes are common in most racquet sports and the mechanics are very similar, wrist action sometimes differs from sport to sport.

BASIC GRIPS

A number of different grips are used to hold the racquet. The decision on which grip to employ is based on the individual player's preference and on body position and ball position in the game situation. The grips include the eastern forehand, the eastern backhand, and the continental. The grip should be comfortable and provide freedom of movement for the wrist, yet allow the fingers to hold the racquet firmly, like a door-knob grip, so that it does not turn in the hand.

For the eastern forehand, place the nonhitting hand on the throat of the racquet with the racquet head lengthwise, in a vertical position to the floor. Reach down and shake hands with the grip as shown in Figure 5.1. The butt of the racquet handle is even with the base of your

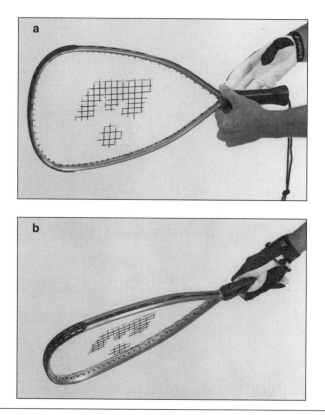

Figure 5.1   Assuming the eastern forehand grip: Hold the racquet by the throat (a) and reach down to shake hands with the racquet (b).

hand, and the V formed between the thumb and the index finger (see Figure 5.2) runs down through the top flat section of the handle. The fingers are usually together around the handle, although you may prefer to spread the index finger. Do not place the index finger behind the handle as a brace—your finger is not strong enough to brace the racquet. You lose control of the grip and get much more racquet rotation with the index finger used as a brace. The forehand grip can also be achieved by placing the hand, palm down, against the racquet face, which is held vertically to the ground, and then sliding the hand down the throat to the handle to grip the racquet.

The eastern backhand grip is the same as the eastern forehand grip except that you rotate the racquet, with grip fingers relaxed, about one quarter inch to the right (to the left for left-handed players) and regrip it. The V formed between the thumb and index finger is now over the small beveled edge of the racquet handle as shown in Figure 5.3.

For the continental grip, grasp the handle anywhere between the eastern forehand and eastern backhand grips. Because the change from eastern forehand to eastern backhand is slight, the continental grip is actually a variation of the other grips. Although most players change from the forehand to the backhand grip during the game,

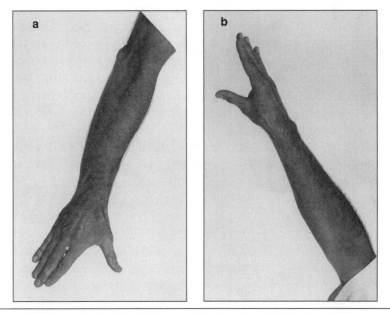

Figure 5.2 Two views of the V between the thumb and index finger. The proper racquet handle location of the V changes depending on which grip you use.

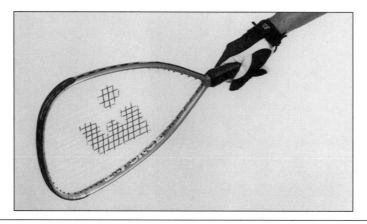

Figure 5.3   The eastern backhand grip.

some players employ the continental grip for both forehands and backhands because this grip does not have to be changed at any time. The continental grip is especially useful when there is not enough time to change the grip and you must hit a backhand shot with a forehand grip or vice versa. Although using the continental grip helps to avoid these awkward situations, we recommend that you change grips for forehands and backhands whenever possible.

Beginners may find it helpful to mark their grip pattern on the racquet. Do this by painting the palm and fingers of the grip hand with contrasting latex paint. Then grip the handle of the racquet, hold it for 15 seconds, and release the hand. You now have a pattern on your racquet handle to use for the grip. After the paint dries, use a different color to place a backhand pattern over the forehand pattern. Having a pattern to grip is very helpful for consistently maintaining the correct grip on each hit. Alternatively, tape can be placed in Vs on the handle as patterns for the correct grips. Figure 5.4 shows where your V should be for the various grips we've described.

Some players use a two-handed backhand because it gives them more racquet stability and more power. For the two-handed backhand grip, grasp the handle in the eastern forehand position and place the nonhitting hand above it in a forehand grip. The problem with two-handed grips is that you have a shorter reach and less power from your hitting hand because your leverage has been reduced. However, you gain power overall because the second hand is on the racquet. Most players use a one-handed backhand stroke.

Some advanced players slightly modify the basic grip by sliding the small finger off the racquet. This allows the ring finger to rest on

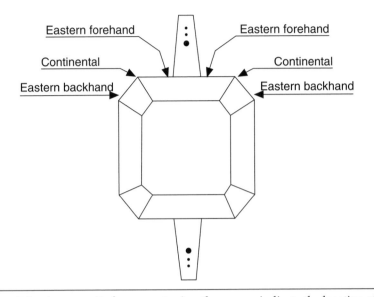

Figure 5.4 A composite for racquet grips: the arrows indicate the location of the V for each grip.

the end of the handle. This increases power because it lengthens the hitting lever (arm and racquet) and it also increases the player's reach. A problem with this adjustment, however, is that a player must have relatively strong fingers and forearms to grip the racquet firmly with only three fingers and the thumb on the handle. If you cannot hold the racquet comfortably with this modified grip, you should use all four fingers on the grip. However, if you can control the racquet with the small finger off the handle, this is an ideal grip to obtain an advantage in power and reach.

HITTING THE STROKES

All sports allow for certain variations in the fundamentals to accommodate specific situations. Racquetball is no different. Information presented on hitting position can be adjusted to suit a particular situation. Here we describe the ideal position for most shots—the position that allows maximum power, fluidity, and control.

First, getting into the basic hitting position requires you to face a side wall. Whether you are hitting a forehand or a backhand shot will determine which side wall you should face. Facing the side wall is the foundation for the basic hitting positions. If you are not facing a side wall, stop yourself and correct your positioning before your next shot. If you have a weak foundation, you can never construct a strong building; it is the same with your basic hitting position. Facing the side wall means that your shoulders are parallel to the side wall. Of course, there are times during play when you don't have time to turn your whole body sideways. Even then you need to turn your upper body so that your shoulders are parallel to the side wall.

In the wall-facing position, you should be crouching slightly with knees bent and with a slightly flexed abdominal area. Bending and flexing allows you to get lower to the ball and helps you keep the ball lower on the front wall. Feet should be slightly wider than shoulder-width apart and shoulders should be level.

The next part of the basic hitting position is the full backswing with the racquet cocked well behind your head. Bend the elbow of the hitting arm about 90 degrees in the backswing position. The hitting arm's elbow and forearm should be about head high. The nonhitting arm is relaxed and pointed back during the backswing, and the nonhitting hand is near the racquet head. The backswing position of the nonhitting arm is the same for both forehand and backhand shots. When done correctly, the backswing position causes the upper body to rotate slightly.

From the full backswing position the upper body begins to move forward. This initial upper body movement helps to create a "pulling factor" for the remainder of the stroke. As the hitting arm moves forward, the upper body continues to rotate forward and the cocked wrist begins to straighten. As the swing continues forward there is a slight lead with the hitting elbow. If you are hitting a forehand shot, the nonhitting arm comes forward and points to the front wall; this helps pull the upper body around more quickly. If you are hitting a backhand shot, the nonhitting arm follows the hitting arm forward but stays close to the body and helps pull the upper body around more quickly. The upper body rotation begins first and is followed by shoulders, elbow, wrist, and racquet in that order.

As the hitting arm comes forward to strike the ball, the arm is almost at full extension. When you make contact, the ball is opposite and in line with the lead hip. The wrist, which was cocked on the backswing and straightened on the forward swing, rotates and flexes at contact and is bent in toward the body.

As forward arm movement and upper body rotation are occurring, the body weight shifts from the rear foot to the front foot, transferring power into the racquet at impact. Normally, the shift of weight takes place by stepping forward with the lead foot. This step is toward the front wall, and the lead foot should be angled toward the front wall at about 45 degrees. It should not be perpendicular or parallel to the front wall. Figure 5.5 shows Woody after he has stepped forward but just before weight transfer (and simultaneous contact with the ball). Notice that he faces the side wall, points backward, and cocks his wrist.

The last major part of the basic hitting position is the follow-through with the racquet. The follow-through should be full and slightly upward. Don't try to stop your follow-through; your body will naturally slow down your arm and stop your follow-through motion. It takes extra strength and energy to unnaturally stop your follow-through.

Throughout the basic hitting sequence, you are always watching the ball and are in position far enough away from the walls so that you can complete a smooth swing. Remember, you are moving very quickly as you perform the hitting sequence. When you complete the shot, you must immediately assume the ready position (shown in Figure 5.6) to await the next shot.

Figure 5.5 Woody showing proper forehand form.

Figure 5.6   The body should be bent and low in the ready position.

GENERATING POWER

Ultimate power comes from combining many sources of power at racquet-ball impact. The hitter needs to employ all of these sources to achieve maximum velocity. First and most important, you must be in the side position, facing the wall, to make use of all the power sources. Remember, power beginning with the upper body and legs is increased by the other aspects of the swing, but if your body is not in the side position to start with, you cannot achieve maximum force on the ball. Assuming the correct position allows you to use two components of racquetball hitting power: overall upper and lower body strength and the elements of the swing that maximize racquet speed. The first and major source of power is upper body rotation from the hip area. Rotation of the upper body during this part of the hitting sequence pulls with it many of the other sources of power. The body pulls the arm, the elbow, the wrist, and the racquet around.

The backswing and the follow-through are two essential sources of power. You need a full backswing, with a cocked racquet, bent elbow that is about head high, along with a full follow-through. Remember that the follow-through stops naturally because of normal range of motion; do not consciously stop or shorten your natural follow-through.

A fourth source of power is the wrist rotation-flexion that occurs just before and during racquet-ball impact. Flexion-rotation is the bending and turning of the cocked wrist to achieve maximum hitting force as a result of moving the wrist through the greatest range of motion. As you advance in skill, wrist flexion-rotation becomes an ever greater source of hitting power. Wrist flexion-rotation is commonly known as wrist snap.

Shifting body weight by transferring the weight from the back leg and foot to the front leg and foot is yet another source of power. You can shift weight while hitting either by taking a step or by changing the point of balance from rear to front.

The sixth source of power is arm action during the swing. On the backswing the hitting arm is bent. As you bring the arm forward through the swing, the elbow leads slightly and then the arm almost

---

Key Elements for Grips and Basic Hitting Position

- Use the eastern forehand grip on forehand shots and change to an eastern backhand grip when hitting a backhand.
- Be sure that you have the correct grip and that you wrap your index finger around the handle rather than extend it up the back of the handle as a brace.
- Face a side wall when hitting the ball.
- Hit from a semicrouched position.
- For hitting forehands the nonhitting arm should extend, after ball contact, toward the front wall; on backhands the nonhitting arm should move forward close to the body during the whole swing.
- Use a full backswing and rotate the upper body so that your shoulders are open to the back wall.
- Step forward toward the front wall and shift the weight from the back foot to the front foot.
- Remember, your body becomes a power unit with all sources of power combining at ball-racquet impact.

Table 5.1   Power Summary Chart

Upper-body rotation	On backswing, shoulders rotated toward back wall; shoulders and upper body rotated forward during swing.
Backswing and follow-through	Full swing, head-high elbow, bent-arm backswing with cocked racquet; full arm extension during follow-through.
Shift of body weight	The weight shifts from the back leg and foot to the front leg and foot; take a step or shift point of balance from back to front.
Leg extension	Both legs are bent in basic ready position; they partially extend and straighten during racquet-ball impact.
Arm swing	The arm is bent during the backswing; elbow leads and arm extends during swing and impact.
Wrist rotation-flexion	The wrist is cocked before impact; it straightens, bends, and turns during impact.
Abdominal area	Abdominal area is flexed in ready position; it straightens and uncoils as the racquet strikes the ball.
Nonhitting arm	On both forehands and backhands, the nonhitting arm adds speed to upper body rotation.
Power unit	All sources are cumulative at racquet-ball contact.

fully extends at racquet-ball impact. The elbow lead and arm extension add power to the shot.

The legs play a role as the seventh source of power. Remember, at the start of the basic hitting position, you are crouching with the legs bent, and when the racquet strikes the ball, you partially extend the legs. Partially extending and straightening your legs adds more body force to the shot. Normally, the front leg is partially extended, and the back leg is fully extended. The back foot pivots so that it is pointing to the front wall, and you are on the ball of this foot and likewise on the ball of the front foot.

The eighth power source is the abdominal area, which is slightly flexed in the basic ready position. As the upper body rotates forward during the swing, the abdominal area straightens—an uncoiling action—and adds power to the shot.

The ninth and last source of power comes from the nonhitting arm. For both forehand and backhand shots, the nonhitting arm is back near the racquet in the backswing phase of the hit. For the forehand shot, the nonhitting arm comes forward and extends as the upper body rotates. As the nonhitting arm extends, it helps pull the upper body around farther, thus increasing upper body speed and hitting power. On backhand shots, the nonhitting arm comes forward with the swing but stays close to the body. It does not extend forward as in the forehand shot. During the follow-through, the arm stays bent across the chest.

All nine components must come together at racquet-ball impact or your shot will be weaker than it should be. If you find you're not hitting clean, crisp shots with authority, look over the Power Summary Chart to see where you could be losing power.

Drills for Basic Hitting

Grip Drill

Purpose:

To practice proper racquet grips and to obtain a feel of racquet-ball impact.

Directions:

Stand anywhere in the court, use the correct forehand grip, and bounce the ball on the floor using the forehand face of the racquet. Bounce the ball waist high (25 repetitions).

Variations:

A. Use a backhand grip and the backhand face of the racquet to bounce the ball waist high.

B. Use both forehand and backhand grips and bounce the ball up, rather than down, off the correct racquet face. Bounce the ball two to three feet high.

Basic Side Position Drill

Purpose:

To practice the proper side-hitting position.

Directions:

In a semicrouched position, stand facing the forehand side wall near the center of the court; drop the ball low (about six to twelve inches from the floor); let it bounce; and hit it to the front wall (50 repetitions).

Variations:

A. Stand facing the backhand side wall and drop and hit the ball to the front wall.

B. Stand facing a side wall near the back of the court and drop and hit the ball to the front wall using both forehand and backhand shots.

C. Stand facing a side wall and bounce the ball to the floor so that it will hit the side wall you are facing. Allow the ball to bounce on the floor again and then hit forehand and backhand shots.

Chapter 6

Hitting Passing Shots and Kills

Photo by Stan Badz—KILLSHOT magazine

*T*wo of the most common and effective shots in racquetball are passing and kill shots. Unlike specialty shots described in chapter 10, the passing and kill shots are hit with normal forehand or backhand strokes and are intended to end a rally. Your success with these shots depends upon how well you develop the basic hitting skills described in chapter 5. If you are patient and have good hitting position and swinging mechanics, you will hit effective passing and kill shots.

PASSING SHOTS

The passing shot is the most versatile shot in racquetball and is one of the two best offensive weapons. Unlike the kill shot, which requires pinpoint accuracy, a passing shot can be effective even though it lacks perfect placement. You can use the passing shot to move your opponent out of center court into the backcourt so that you can gain center-court advantage. Unlike the kill shot, which ends a point immediately, the passing shot can end a point and wear down your opponents by making them run. Two views of Woody about to hit a passing shot are shown in Figure 6.1. Note the high backswing with a bent elbow and eyes on the ball.

Figure 6.1   Woody bends his elbow and uses a high backswing as he prepares for (a) passing shot and (b) backwall passing shot.

Shot Strategy

As the name implies, the passing shot is a shot that should go past your opponent. Because the passing shot is an offensive weapon, the strategy is either to win a point outright or to force your opponent to hit a weak return. Two factors determine when to use the passing shot: your position and your opponent's position. Normally, passing shots are hit a) when you are back and your opponent is forward, b) when you and your opponent are on the same side of the court, or c) when you are on one side of the court and your opponent is on the other side. Passing shots are not very good when you are forward in the court, although at times you can hit an effective pass from this position.

The passing shot has two elements: The ball goes by your opponent and it takes its second bounce before it ends in a back corner. Although accuracy is important, you must hit with enough speed to ensure that the ball goes past your opponent. The passing shot should hit the front wall approximately two to five feet from the floor so that the ball will take a quick second bounce and will not rebound off the back wall into center court. If a passing shot strikes the front wall higher than this, your opponent can usually return it. In addition, hit the ball almost parallel to the floor and use enough power on the shot to pass your opponent. However, don't use too much power on a high passing shot. This causes the ball to rebound out of the corner or off the back wall toward center court before it takes its second bounce. Remember that the passing shot is an offensive weapon. The three basic passing shots include the crosscourt, the down-the-wall, and the wide-angle shot, and each shot is used in a different situation.

Going Crosscourt

If you and your opponent are on the same side of the court, as seen in Figure 6.2, hit the crosscourt passing shot. The ball should hit near the center of the front wall and angle back across the court to the far back corner.

Shooting Down-the-Wall

If you are on one side of the court and your opponent is on the other side, as seen in Figure 6.3, hit the passing shot directly into the front wall so that the ball rebounds along the wall nearest to you, stays parallel to the wall, and ends in the back corner closest to you. Because the ball travels along the wall during this shot, it is called the down-the-wall passing shot. It may also be called a parallel passing shot or a down-the-line passing shot.

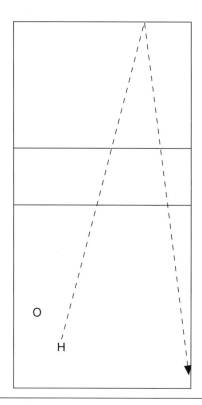

Figure 6.2 The crosscourt pass.

The Wide-Angle Pass

The wide-angle passing shot is a regular passing shot hit at a wider than normal angle. It can put a little extra distance between the ball and your opponent. That distance can sometimes make the difference between a successful and an unsuccessful pass. The wide-angle pass is a modified crosscourt passing shot. Like the other passing shots, the wide-angle is designed to place the ball in a back corner. When you hit the wide-angle pass, try to strike the front wall at an angle that makes the ball rebound to the far side wall even with or slightly behind your opponent, as shown in Figure 6.4. The wider angle causes the ball, as it comes off the side wall, to rebound across the court past and away from your opponent. For the wide-angle pass to be successful, your opponent must be no farther back than

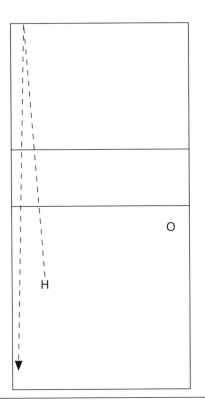

Figure 6.3   The down-the-wall pass.

center court. If he or she is behind center court, the ball will rebound off the side wall to your opponent.

Accuracy is essential for an effective wide-angle passing shot; if you miscalculate only slightly, the ball will either rebound directly to your opponent or it will go into the back wall and come out as an easy setup. This problem results from hitting the ball too high or too far behind your opponent on the side wall. The target on the side wall is a two-foot area opposite or slightly behind your opponent; hitting this spot ensures success of the wide-angle shot especially if the ball hits the side wall no more than a few feet from the floor. If you can hit the shot low enough, the ball merely rolls out from the side wall-floor crack. It is important to remember that passing shots are best executed when your opponent is somewhere in the front two thirds of the court. Concentrate on accuracy rather than speed.

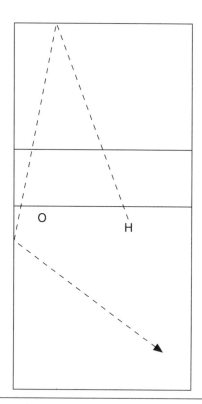

Figure 6.4 The wide-angle pass.

Backhand Passing Shots

Backhand passing shots are essentially the same as forehand passing shots. For beginning and intermediate players, foot positioning is important in all backhand shots. Figure 6.5 shows Woody's foot positioning and backswing preparation. In a backhand down-the-wall pass, the lead foot steps straight ahead with the toes pointing to the near front corner. With a crosscourt backhand pass, your lead foot points a little more toward the front-wall side of the near corner. In addition, you may strike the ball slightly in front of your lead foot on the backhand pass. Many players are concerned about their backhands and have a tendency to let up on this shot. Hitting slightly in front of the lead foot gives you an aggressive shot.

If both you and your opponent are right-handed, your forehand crosscourt pass will be very effective because it will end in the

Figure 6.5   Woody in position for the backhand passing shot.

backhand corner of your opponent. The same is true of your backhand down-the-wall passing shot. Conversely, your backhand crosscourt pass and your forehand down-the-wall pass will end in your opponent's forehand back corner. (Of course, the reverse is true if your opponent is left-handed.) This concept assumes that the backhand is weaker than the forehand.

You should pay attention to the distance the ball travels on passing shots. On the down-the-wall passing shot, the ball travels a shorter distance than a crosscourt passing shot hit from the same place. This means that a down-the-wall shot gives your opponent less time to return the ball, and you have greater accuracy because of the shorter distance the ball travels.

Except for the wide-angle passing shot, the ball should never hit the side wall near center court or rebound out from the back wall near center court. To avoid hitting the side wall, change your angle of front-wall contact, hit lower, or hit with a little less force.

Key Elements for the Passing Shot
• Hit the ball low enough and slow enough that it will not rebound off the back wall.
• Hit the ball away from your opponent; choose your passing shot considering your position and your opponent's position.
• On crosscourt shots, you may hit the side wall as long as it is toward the back of the court.
• On down-the-wall shots, hit the ball at an angle to the front wall so that the ball never hits a side wall.
• On wide-angle passing shots, angle the ball against the front wall so that it hits the side wall opposite or behind your opponent.

KILL SHOTS

The kill shot is *the* offensive shot in racquetball. When the kill shot is hit well, it is the most lethal shot in the game and is never returned by your opponent. Your satisfaction is derived from winning the point, keeping the ball low, and not allowing your opponent a chance to retrieve the ball.

Shot Strategy

The key in hitting the kill shot is to keep the ball low on the front wall. If the ball is kept low on the front wall, as seen in Figure 6.6, it will take its second bounce very quickly and be impossible to return. The perfect kill is a *roll-out*, a ball that hits so low on the front wall that it actually rolls across the floor.

Hit Low

Several elements are needed to keep the ball low on the front wall. One factor is patience. You need to wait on the ball so that when your racquet makes contact, the ball is below knee level. Usually, the lower the ball when you hit it, the lower it will stay on the front wall. Beginners tend to become excited and play the ball too soon and, therefore, find it difficult to consistently keep their kill shots down.

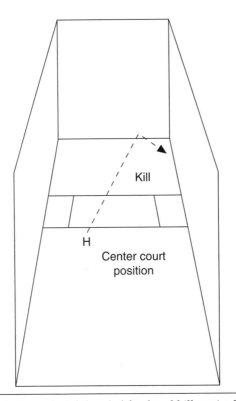

Figure 6.6   The trajectory of a left-handed forehand kill; notice how low the ball hits the front wall.

Once you learn patience, the next important requirement is to get your body down to the height of the ball by bending your knees. Bending the knees and getting the body low is difficult for most players. Be sure you are facing a side wall when preparing to hit a kill. When you bend your legs, remember also to lower your butt. To achieve this low position with a good base of support, you must put yourself into a modified lunge position, with the lead leg bent under the body and the back leg slightly more extended behind the body. This modified lunge position is the most efficient way of lowering your center of gravity and thus lowering your body.

To keep the ball low, the racquet head should be pointed toward the side wall; it should not be pointed toward the floor. If the head is pointing to the floor, chances are good that the racquet face will be angled back slightly, and the ball will rise slightly after impact. If the head is pointing to a side wall, the face should remain flat and the ball should stay low and straight after impact.

All basic hitting procedures described in previous chapters apply to hitting the kill successfully. However, a few new points need to be highlighted. Because you need to be watching the ball, your head should be close to the floor when you hit the kill. Lowering your head helps keep the ball lower on the front wall; when you raise your head, the racquet and your body are lifted at the same time. To kill effectively from deep in the backcourt, you must hit the shot with considerable power. Of course, you first must achieve accuracy. Once accuracy is established, you should work on hitting the ball with power. The best kill shot is hit from ankle to knee high. Timing your swing and racquet-ball contact is important for good kill shots since there is a small margin of error between a good kill shot and a skipped ball.

Position Yourself for the Kill

If you are a beginning or intermediate player, hit your kills when you are in frontcourt or center court and your opponent is deep in the court. This position puts you closer to the front wall where the shorter distance will increase your accuracy. With your opponent back, even if you hit the ball a little too high, the chances of a return are slim. If you are back and your opponent is forward, your kill shot must be perfect or it is likely to be returned. See Figure 6.7 for the best court position to hit kills.

Hit Level

A fundamental law of physics is that for every action there is an equal and opposite reaction. If you play a ball above the knee and attempt to hit it low on the front wall, there is a good chance it will rebound high off the floor, and your opponent will have enough time to get the ball. Therefore, if you attempt to kill a high ball, you lower your success percentage.

Hitting kill shots at the improper place causes the ball to hit the floor, or skip, before it hits the front wall. Skipping the ball on a straight kill shot can result from contacting the ball behind the midline of your body. In this position your racquet face naturally closes and causes the ball to skip. A skipped ball can also be caused by hitting even with your midline with a closed racquet face. If your grip is causing the closed face, adjust your grip. Finally, a kill shot can skip because of a lack of power. When hitting the ball this low, if you lack sufficient power to propel the ball quickly, it will hit the floor before hitting the front wall. Check your power sources.

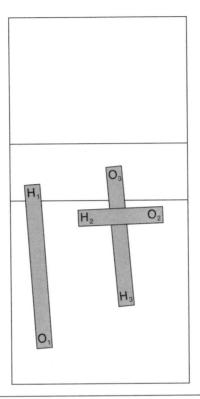

Figure 6.7   The best hitting position for the kill is when the hitter is at H_1 and the opponent is at O_1. Position H_2 and O_2 is less ideal, and position H_3 and O_3 is even more dicey.

Front-Wall Kills

The straight front-wall kill can be hit down-the-wall or crosscourt. The front-wall kill is shown in Figure 6.8. If the down-the-wall or crosscourt kill is hit too high, it becomes a good passing shot, but if it's too low, it will skip. You can also hit overhead kills, but this is a lower percentage shot and will be discussed in chapter 10.

Kill shots are most effective when you are in center court and your opponent is behind you. They are a good choice when your opponent hits a short ceiling shot and when the opponent's ball rebounds off the back wall near the center-court area.

Pinch and Reverse-Pinch Kills

Pinch and reverse-pinch kills work the front corners of the court. They are also referred to as corner kills. A corner kill that hits the side wall and then the front wall is a pinch kill. A reverse pinch hits the front wall first and then ricochets off the side walls as seen in Figure 6.9. You may hit both near-corner pinches and far-corner pinches. Pinches can be hit as both forehand and backhand shots. The splat is another form of a corner kill. Both splats and pinches are discussed in more depth in chapter 10.

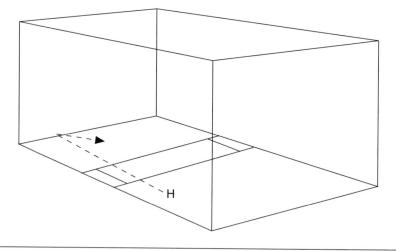

Figure 6.8 The basic straight front-wall kill.

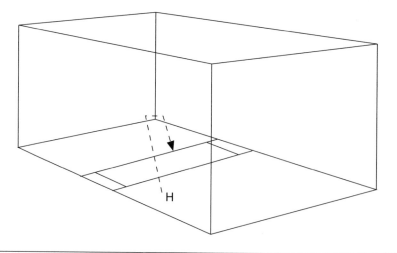

Figure 6.9 The crosscourt corner kill.

Key Elements for the Kill Shot

- Hit the ball low on the front wall by bending your knees and lowering your center of gravity.
- Be patient and allow the ball to come close to the floor before you play it.
- You must develop a comfort zone about where you contact the ball on a kill shot. Usually this zone is knee high or lower.
- Keep your racquet head parallel and flat and keep your head down.
- Develop accuracy first, speed and power second.

Taking Your Game to Its Highest Level   *Woody Clouse*

Passing shots are the highest percentage offensive shots in the game.

- Passing shots have the greatest margin for error; therefore, they have the highest chance for success.
- You will always force your opponent out of center court.
- You will be given the necessary time to set yourself in center court.
- You will force your opponent to hit the ball off balance and out of position.

As a rule of thumb, you should only hit a kill or a pinch when you believe that the shot will end the rally. If not, continue using passing shots. When you kill or pinch, one of three things will happen:

- You will nail the shot and win the rally.
- You will skip the ball.
- You will leave the ball up, giving your opponent a setup in the center of the court.

Obviously the percentages are not going to be in your favor if you kill and pinch the ball too much.

(continued)

- The best time to hit a kill or pinch is when you are up front and your opponent is deep in the backcourt. This forces your opponent to run around the court to retrieve the shot. You are also legally obstructing the opponent's view when you hit the shot with your opponent back.

Drills for the Passing Shot

Paper Bag Drill

Purpose:
To practice passing-shot selection.

Directions:
Place an empty paper grocery bag upright in the court as your opponent. Place the bag in the frontcourt or center court and position yourself in different locations in the backcourt; drop the ball and hit the passing shot dictated by your position and that of your opponent. Reposition the bag to change your shots (30 repetitions at each spot).

Back and Forth Drill

Purpose:
To practice hitting passing shots with a rebounding ball.

Directions:
Position yourself in various backcourt locations, hit the ball to the front wall so that it rebounds back to you, and attempt to hit various passing shots off the rebound (50 repetitions at each spot).

Variations:
   A. Hit the ball away from yourself so that you must move to the ball and hit the passing shot off the rebound.

   B. Have a partner hit the ball to you and practice passing shots off your partner's hit.

   C. Stand near the back wall, toss the ball gently underhanded and low to the back wall, let it bounce, and hit various passing shots both backhand and forehand.

Rally Drill

Purpose:
To practice hitting passing shots with a rebounding ball.

Directions:
Position yourself in various backcourt and midcourt locations, hit the ball to the front wall so that it rebounds back to you, and attempt to hit various passing shots off the rebound (30 repetitions each spot).

Variations:
A. Hit the ball away from yourself so that you must move to the ball and hit the passing shot off the rebound.

B. Have a partner hit the ball to you and practice passing shots off your partner's hit.

Drills for the Kill Shot

Paper Cup Drill

Purpose:
To practice hitting kill shots with a lower stationary ball.

Directions:
Turn a paper cup upside down within the service zone, place the ball on top of the inverted cup, and hit the ball off the cup. It is important to hit the cup as you hit the ball; otherwise you will hit up on the ball. This is an excellent drill because the ball is both low and stationary. Hit forehand, backhand, and other variations of the kill. Begin with a large size (32 ounce) cup (30 repetitions at each spot).

Variations:
A. Use a smaller cup to play the ball lower.

B. Move the cup farther back in the court to make the drill more difficult.

Drop and Hit Drill

Purpose:
To practice hitting kill shots from the service area with a low setup.

Directions:
Stand in the service area facing a side wall, drop the ball low (about six to eight inches from the ground), and hit forehand and backhand straight frontwall kills (25 repetitions from each spot).

Variations:
  A. Hit front-wall—side-wall kill shots and side-wall—front-wall kill shots.

  B. From within the service area, stand near a side wall; toss the ball gently, underhanded, and low to the side wall; let it bounce; and hit various backhand and forehand kill shots.

  C. Move near the back wall; toss the ball gently, underhanded, and low to the back wall; let it bounce; and hit various back hand and forehand kill shots.

Hit and Kill Drill

Purpose:
To hit kill shots off a ball rebounding from the front wall.

Directions:
Stand in the center-court area, hit the ball slowly to the front wall, let the ball bounce one or more times, and return the ball to the front wall with a kill shot (25 repetitions).

Variation:
Position your body to one side of center court and near the back wall; hit and kill.

Low-Ball Kill Drill

Purpose:
To practice obtaining your low kill-shot hitting zone.

Directions:
Stand anywhere in the court, drop and hit the ball low on the front wall, allow it to rebound and bounce so that it is knee height or lower, and attempt to kill the ball (25 repetitions).

Variation:
Allow the ball to go by you, hit the back wall and come forward, and then play it with a kill when it is knee height or lower.

Chapter 7

Hitting Back-Wall, Volley, and Ceiling Shots

Several specialty racquetball shots can be used offensively and defensively when you are caught in particular situations. Although these specialty shots require well-developed skills, you need not be a top-level player to learn them. Moreover, learning these shots will improve your play and allow you to compete with more advanced players. Using these strategic shots indicates that you have advanced your skill level and that you understand racquetball strategy.

BACK-WALL SHOTS

A back-wall shot is simply playing a ball that has traveled to the back wall and is heading toward the front wall as shown in Figure 7.1. The back-wall shot is not a particular type of stroke; rather, it is a strategic way to use other strokes. You can hit forehand or backhand passing, kill, and ceiling shots off the back wall. Any ball played directly off the back wall is considered a back-wall shot. Body position and stroking actions are the same for back-wall shots as for front-wall shots.

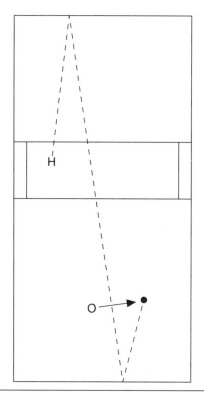

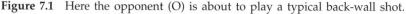

Figure 7.1   Here the opponent (O) is about to play a typical back-wall shot.

One reason for using the back-wall shot is that the ball is traveling toward the front wall. You do not have to change the direction of the ball at impact, you have good control, and you can impart more power to the shot. You can play the ball lower and you have more time since the ball goes by you and then comes back off the wall.

Speed and Angles

The advanced player considers the back-wall shot an easy shot because the ball is set up for a good return. For the beginner, however, the back-wall shot is not easy. The ball is difficult to judge because of its speed and various rebounding angles. Beginners have two major problems in playing back-wall shots. First, as shown by Woody in Figure 7.2, the beginner often plays a high overhand shot

Figure 7.2 Don't play the ball this high. Allow it to go by and then take a back-wall shot.

rather than letting the ball go past to the back wall, and thus loses the opportunity to play an easy back-wall shot. Beginners need patience on all high balls; they should allow fast high balls to go past and then play the ball off the back wall. Of course, a slow-moving high ball should be taken before it gets to the back wall. This slow ball might not rebound off the back wall, which would put the hitter into a defensive rather than offensive position. The decision to allow a ball to go past you to the back wall must be made well before the ball goes past. You need to look at many high balls in practice so you know which to take before the back wall and which to let pass.

In addition, beginners should not be overaggressive on back-wall shots. This tendency can result in playing the wrong high balls and in hitting defensive rather than offensive back-wall shots. Figure 7.3 shows Woody correctly hitting a back-wall shot. Note the backswing (preparation), the point of contact, and the follow-through.

One final point for beginners to remember is to avoid running into the back wall when attempting back-wall shots. It can be unsafe as well as embarrassing. If, for example, you are retreating from center court for a back-wall-off-a-ceiling ball, you should reach behind

Figure 7.3 Woody showing the proper preparation (a), contact (b), and follow-through (c) for a backhand back-wall shot.

yourself with your nonhitting hand to feel for the wall while you concentrate on watching the ball.

Timing and Positioning

A second major problem beginners have is timing and positioning, two problems so closely related that we would like to treat them together. Many beginners follow the ball with the body rather than anticipating where the ball will bounce. If you are constantly running to keep up with the ball, you will be out of position on many shots. However, following the ball with your eyes and anticipating where it is going to rebound will allow you to move to the rebounding spot in time to obtain good position. While moving into position or turning your body, you should never lose sight of the ball.

Because most back-wall shots force you to move backward to meet the ball, speed becomes an important factor in positioning yourself properly. The best way to retreat quickly is as follows. Turn to the side where the ball is passing you and step toward the back wall with the foot on the ball side. Then, cross over the lead foot with your other foot and run sideways into position. Both backpedaling and shuffling to the side are stable movement patterns but give you less time to get into the proper position. Turning completely around and running will cause you to lose sight of the ball.

Always stay in a semicrouched, low position as you move to the ball. Also, starting your backswing almost simultaneously with the body turn for back-wall shots gets the racquet back early, helps to avoid rushing the swing, and aids in a smoother stroking action.

As with all shots, you must move to the ball, stop and get set, and strike. This means you must learn to judge ball speed and ball angles, and practice is the only way to learn. However, back-wall shots are slightly different because you may need to move back to get the ball, you may stay put, or you may have to move forward to play a hard-hit back-wall shot. If you are moving forward, you will be simultaneously moving and hitting toward the front wall; therefore, timing becomes a major concern. The benefit of moving forward as you contact the ball is that you hit the ball with more force because of your momentum toward the front wall. However, you must understand the difficulty of correct timing and positioning while attempting to hit on the run. You must anticipate where the back-wall ball will end up and then move to that position to play the ball.

BB Back-Wall

Sometimes your opponent hits a back-wall shot so hard that you must move to within a few feet of the front wall before you can play the ball. This is called the BB back-wall shot. What do you do with the ball when you are this close to the front wall? You have several options including a drop shot (see chapter 10), a kill, and a passing shot. Your opponent's position will dictate which of the shots you should use. If your opponent is deep in the backcourt, then the drop shot or the kill would be appropriate. If he or she is in center court, use the passing shot. Remembering the proper strategy will help you avoid losing points on BB back-wall shots.

Ceiling and Corner Back-Wall Shots

Two other back-wall shots, the back-wall ceiling ball and the corner ball, require a slightly different hitting technique. When playing a back-wall shot coming from a ceiling ball, remember that the ball is rebounding both down and away from the back wall. Note Woody in Figure 7.4 watching the ball and using his back hand to feel the back wall. Normally, you will need to position yourself closer to the back wall for the ceiling-to-back-wall ball because it will not rebound forward nearly as far as a standard back-wall shot. The key factors in the back-wall-off-a-ceiling shot are to get low and to get behind the ball.

With the corner shots, remember that a ball might take a thousand or more different angles out of the corners. As a ball is approaching the corner, you need to decide which wall the ball is going to strike first. You will position yourself differently on a back-wall first hit as compared to a side-wall first hit. This is an extremely important decision for effective back-wall corner play. Three pointers for back-wall corner shots are (a) be patient and wait for the ball until it gets low, (b) stay at least arm plus racquet length from the corner, and (c) practice so that you learn about corner angles and rebounding. Figure 7.5 shows Woody playing a corner back-wall ball. Note his low body position and how far he is from the corner. The more you play, the more angles you will learn and the better you will be able to react. (Even after years of practice, however, the best players occasionally misplay a corner back-wall shot.) Another good return off a back-wall corner shot is a ceiling shot because it will give you time to get out of a back corner and into better court position.

Figure 7.4 Woody feels for the back wall as he positions himself to return a ceiling-to-back-wall shot.

Figure 7.5 Woody plays the corner back-wall shot. He stays low and remains an arm plus a racquet's length away from the corner.

Back-Wall—Back-Wall

The last of the back-wall shots is when the hitter turns and hits the ball back into the back wall rather than hitting it directly to the front wall. The back-wall—back-wall shot is not desirable because it is mainly defensive. The ball is going up, it is hit in the opposite direction of the front wall, and it must travel a great distance to the front wall—all of which make it a defensive shot. This shot is most often used by beginners. Beginners often feel uncomfortable with their backhands, so they turn and hit to the back wall with a forehand, thus avoiding a backhand shot. Sometimes the back-wall—back-wall shot is used as a last-ditch effort to hit the ball, normally a result of being out of position. Although beginners use the shot more often than intermediate and advanced players, all players must sometimes use back-wall—back-wall shots.

To hit the shot properly, you need to be in position as if you were hitting a regular back-wall shot, except that now you are oriented toward the back wall instead of the front wall. All other aspects of hitting mechanics are the same as for other strokes. Hitting the ball with great force is important because it must travel farther than a typical back-wall shot. Finally, you must hit the back-wall—back-wall shot with an upward swing. This accomplishes two things: First and most important, hitting upward causes the ball to go up to the ceiling and gives you more time to obtain center court; and second, it prevents the ball from rebounding directly into your body. Remember, the back-wall—back-wall shot is not a desirable shot. We suggest using your backhand rather than a back-wall—back-wall shot.

VOLLEY

Volleying, or playing the ball in the air before it bounces, rapidly changes the pace of the game, adding a new dimension to it. Because beginners are often impatient and not used to waiting for the ball, they usually hit the volley at the wrong time and in the wrong manner. This part of the chapter describes in detail the basics of playing the volley, including court position, strategies, and the mechanics of hitting the shot, but let's begin with a few observations.

First, the volley is an offensive weapon, not a defensive shot. They are played most effectively when you are in center court or the frontcourt where they are easier to hit and from where they give your opponent less time to react. Although you can play a volley from the backcourt, it is less effective offensively the farther you move from the front wall. Because you must react quickly to play the volley, you may be hitting from an awkward position. Always try to play the

Key Elements for the Back-Wall Shot

- Begin your racquet backswing early to have more time to stroke the back-wall shot.

- Be patient and allow high balls to go by you and then play them with a back-wall shot.

- Never lose eye contact with the ball when playing back-wall shots.

- Be patient on your back-wall shot and contact the ball low to the floor.

- Hit backhand back-wall shots rather than back-wall—back-wall shots.

- To obtain more force when hitting the ball, play the ball opposite the front hip, not behind the body.

- Learn ball speeds and angles through constant practice.

Taking Your Game to Its Highest Level   *Woody Clouse*

The most important factor in taking a ball off the back wall is setting your feet properly.

- Once your feet are set, your racquet needs to be in the ready position.

- You then need to let the ball drop to around knee level.

- The shot you take should be the one you need to end the rally.

- Back-wall setups are open opportunities to hit winners—go for it!

volley low for an underhand or sidearm shot rather than an over-hand shot.

If your opponent is scrambling and out of position, playing a volley will make his or her situation worse because the volley allows less time to react and increases the pressure. You can play the volley off the front wall or the side wall; both shots are effective. The side-wall shot gives you more time to react, but you have to cope with new angles. The front-wall volley permits you less reaction time, but you have a straight hit to the front wall with no rebound angles to worry about.

You can return a volley straight to the front wall or you can return it to a corner hitting the front wall/side wall or side wall/front wall. The corner or pinch volley is extremely effective in that it affords more angles to which your opponent must react.

Get Into Position

As with all other shots, you should be facing a side wall when hitting the volley. Of course, this is often difficult because you have little time to react to the oncoming ball. Attempt to play the ball to the side of the body rather than the front of the body. If you do not have time to turn sideways completely, you should rotate your upper body so that your shoulders are parallel to a side wall. This stance is a more open position than the side-facing stance. The weight should be on the balls of the feet. Because of the time factor, you will normally not take a step up as you hit the volley shot. Beginners need a tight grip on the racquet when playing a volley because of the speed of the ball at impact. Intermediate and advanced players should use the standard firm grip for volleys.

Hit Low

One of the most important aspects of a successful volley is to play the ball low, and the ideal place to contact the ball is below the waist. Figure 7.6a shows Woody playing the ball low by bending his knees to lower his center of gravity. Figure 7.6b shows the improper position to hit a volley: Woody is bending at the waist instead of bending his knees. Above-the-waist volleys are somewhat less effective than volleys played below the waist because of the difficulty of holding the racquet high and hitting with much power or control. In

Figure 7.6 The correct (a) and incorrect (b) form for volleying.

fact, the volley backswing and follow-through generally tend to be somewhat shortened because of the lack of time for pivoting, and the shot is mainly a punch or a block. In any case, remember to contact the ball below the waist.

Hit Quickly

A few additional maneuvers will help you hit an effective volley. First, watch your opponent set up for his or her shot so that you can gain additional time to maneuver into position. In addition, you should keep your racquet low, about midthigh, with the head still pointing to a side wall. Because volleying decreases reaction time for both you and your opponent, any time advantage you can gain counts.

You should also remember that volleying permits you to maintain center-court position (rather than running to the backcourt to play the same ball off the back wall). Holding center court means that you'll use less energy to make your shots, and in very long games this is a decided advantage. Finally, because the volley is a dominating shot, play it aggressively, place it low and straight to the front wall or to a corner, and use it to put your opponent away.

Hit a Variety of Shots

You may use the volley to play kill shots, passing shots, pinch shots, drop shots, and ceiling shots. Kill shots and passing shots are the easiest shots to master using the volley. The pinch shot takes precise timing, and the ceiling shot is very difficult to hit off a volley. When a ceiling shot is played, it is normally an offensive shot because you use it to maintain center-court or frontcourt positioning. Soft midcourt kills, pinch shots, and drop shots (see chapter 10) are also effective off the volley, especially when your opponent is in the backcourt.

It is worth noting that even if you make a slight mistake in executing the volley, you are still in control of center-court position. Another advantage of the volley is that when you make the shot, you are often between the ball and your opponent, and he or she loses sight of the ball. This is a legal visual block.

Finally, if your opponent is driving hard shots at you, don't be intimidated. Try to react as quickly as you can, use the techniques we have been describing, and maintain center court. If you cannot volley a particular ball, let it go by and take it off the back wall. Get back to volleying again as soon as possible; it is one of your best offensive weapons.

CEILING SHOT

The ceiling shot can be used both offensively and defensively. It can be hit underhand, overhand, and with both forehand and backhand strokes. The ceiling ball hits the ceiling first, then the front wall; then it bounces on the floor and lands deep in the backcourt, preferably in a back corner as seen in Figure 7.7.

The ceiling shot is probably the most versatile shot in the game. You can hit it down the wall (wallpaper) or crosscourt; you can hit it off another ceiling ball, off a kill or pass, off back-wall shots, off service returns, or off volleys. In ceiling shots the ball must not hit a side wall; if it does, the ball will go to center court and give your

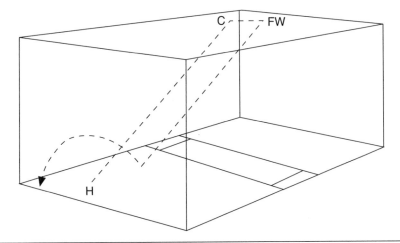

Figure 7.7   A typical ball flight pattern for the ceiling shot.

Key Elements for the Volley

- For better control on your volley, stand facing sideways or rotate your shoulders parallel to a side wall.
- The volley should be played below the waist to hit effective passing and kill shots.
- Keep a firm grip on the racquet at racquet-ball impact. Otherwise the force of the ball will cause the racquet to rotate in your hand and you will lose control of your shot.

Taking Your Game to Its Highest Level

Hitting a volley is a great way to keep your opponent off balance.

- You should volley balls only when you have a good base of support and good balance.
- Hitting pinches off the volley is usually a good shot because your opponent will most likely be deep in the backcourt.
- Make sure you have time to be set; don't rush your shot.
- When hitting the volley make sure to stay down through the entire stroke.

opponent a setup. You will normally use the shot from the backcourt, but a reverse ceiling shot can be effectively played from the midcourt and frontcourt areas. Any serious player must possess a good ceiling shot.

Let's look first at the basic stroke mechanics for successfully executing the shot. Unlike other strokes you do not always need to be facing a side wall when you hit the ceiling shot. The side-facing position does give beginners the power to hit the ball the long distance from the back of the court to the top, to the front, to the floor, and back again to the rear of the court. You obtain power from stepping into the ball, using a large backswing (see Figure 7.8), using follow-through, rotating the upper body, snapping the wrist, extending the leg, and using arm and shoulder power sources. As a beginner you must understand the power requirements of the ceiling shot, and you must incorporate all the elements of proper hitting. The intermediate- and advanced-level players hit with enough force so that touch becomes more important than power. A stiff wrist at ball contact will also help the intermediate and advanced player control the ball better in the ceiling shot. Figure 7.9 shows Woody in the basic contact position for the ceiling shot.

Overhand Ceiling Shot

The overhand ceiling shot is very similar to a partial overhand throw of a ball or the serve in tennis. You reach up and contact the ball at head-level with arm slightly extended. This contact point (as shown in Figure 7.10a) opens the racquet face and propels the ball upward toward the front ceiling. Note that in Figure 7.10b Woody is reaching up high for the ball (a good beginner's technique, but his racquet face is too closed). If you hit the ball too far in front of your body, the ball will never reach the ceiling—your racquet face is too closed—but instead will travel directly to the front wall. If you make contact too far behind the midline of the body, the ball will hit the ceiling but never reach the front wall—your racquet face is too open.

Playing the ball at the middle of the body should allow the proper racquet-face angle to send the ball to an area on the ceiling one foot to six feet from the front wall. This target may vary depending on your court position when you hit the ball, on the liveliness of the ball, and on the playing situation.

Figure 7.8 Woody takes a big backswing as he prepares to launch a ceiling shot.

For beginners, the nonhitting arm should be reaching up on the forehand overhand ceiling shot to almost point at the ball. This improves your concentration and allows the nonhitting arm to act as a lever, pulling your upper body around faster and giving beginners some extra power. Imagine throwing the racquet into the ball; it will help you achieve a fluid action with the overhand ceiling stroke. The amount of power needed on the ball for overhand ceiling shots is minimal for the intermediate and advanced player. Use touch and control to keep the ball in the back corners.

The overhand backhand ceiling shot is hit virtually the same as the overhand forehand ceiling shot. The only difference is the non-hitting arm is only partially extended and remains close to the shoulders and chest on the follow-through. Using all of your power sources is critical, especially for beginners, because, generally, they have much less natural power on their backhand side. Playing the ball as high as possible—going up onto the balls of the feet and the toes—helps to cut down the distance the ball travels and thus gives more speed to the shot.

Figure 7.9   Contact the ball high to hit a ceiling shot.

On all overhand ceiling shots the ball should travel deep to the back of the court and land in a back corner. The ball should hug the side wall or go crosscourt to the opposite back corner. The ball should not rebound from the back wall, but should remain near it. If the ball comes off the back wall or back corner more than a few feet, it becomes an invitation for your opponent to kill; accuracy is therefore as important as power in the ceiling shot.

Underhand Ceiling Shot

All the elements of hitting the overhand ceiling shot with power and accuracy apply to the underhand ceiling shot. Of course, the position of contact is different, but body position is side-facing, and the swing is identical to passing or kill shots until just before ball contact is made. Lower your racquet head to open the racquet face, snap the wrist (this is not a tennis stroke with a shoulder-action swing), and strike the ball opposite or slightly forward of the front hip. Maintain an open racquet face to impart upward trajectory to the ball.

Figure 7.10 For the overhand ceiling shot, reach up and contact the ball at head level (a). Reaching higher up (b) closes the racquet face. Closing the face too far will result in a shot that travels directly to the front wall instead of hitting the ceiling first.

For the intermediate and advanced player, the underhand ceiling shot is mostly a last-ditch effort to return a super shot or is a defensive shot if you're off balance.

Reverse Ceiling Shot

The reverse ceiling shot is a variation of the ceiling shots we have been discussing, and is similar to the regular ceiling shot with two exceptions: First, the ball is hit to the front wall first, to an area approximately two to five feet below the ceiling; second, the ball is hit with high upward trajectory so that after hitting the front wall it then hits the ceiling and travels to the backcourt like a regular ceiling shot, as seen in Figure 7.11. Hitting the front wall before the ceiling—reversing the normal sequence—imparts a great deal of backspin on the ball as it bounces on the floor. The backspin slows down the

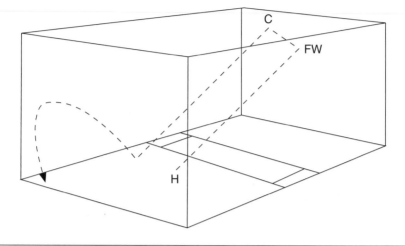

Figure 7.11   The typical ball flight pattern for the reverse ceiling shot.

backward progress of the ball and can create a difficult situation for your opponent, who may expect the ball to be traveling at high speed to the back wall and therefore takes the wrong position to play the ball. Backspin can also make the ball rebound with less force off the back wall, which gives you an effective ceiling shot. However, it may also prevent the ball from reaching the back wall, and thus set up your opponent for a kill.

You normally hit the reverse ceiling shot when you are in the frontcourt along with your opponent. Frontcourt positioning is fairly important in order to achieve the upward trajectory necessary to send the ball high on the front wall and then to the ceiling. From the backcourt it is very difficult to put the proper angle on the ball.

The Ceiling Shot as Offense

The ceiling shot requires power for the beginner and touch for the higher level player. It is important to keep the ball in the backcourt and back corner areas. Let's look at the ceiling shot as an offensive weapon.

The ceiling shot can be used offensively to win a point against an opponent who has difficulty returning high, arching shots. This is a very effective weapon against beginning players. What makes the ceiling shot so effective against beginners? As the ball comes off the back wall or out of the back corners, it is not only coming out but is also traveling downward. This combination of outward and downward flight is often difficult for beginners to judge. A second offensive use of the ceiling shot is to move your opponent out of center court. Once you have done this, you can take center court and utilize offensive strategy. This technique is effective against all players and gives you many offensive shot opportunities.

The Ceiling Shot as Defense

The ceiling shot is defensively important when you are out of position and scrambling to return a ball. It gives you the maximum amount of time to recover and move to good court position while your opponent plays the ball. It is also effective for returning serves, especially power serves, and any other shot that you are digging up while scrambling. The ceiling shot is also a good way to return another ceiling shot. Returning a ceiling shot with a ceiling shot often results in lengthy ceiling-shot rallies that continue until one player makes a mistake and the ball is put away by the opponent. In ceiling-shot rallies, both players remain in the backcourt until an error is made or a new strategy emerges.

When you are in trouble, the ceiling shot is the best percentage shot; if played well, it gives your opponent very little to hit. The ceiling shot can also be used to change the pace, or tempo, of your game. For example, if you and your opponent are both hitting hard shots, changing tempo with the ceiling shot can sometimes be effective in winning a point. A ceiling-ball player can often beat a hard hitter who has not perfected the slower game. A good rule of thumb: If you can't hit an offensive pass or kill shot or you are out of position, go to the ceiling.

The ceiling shot also gives a new dimension to your game—the running dimension. You can run an opponent to exhaustion by intermittently hitting ceiling shots that make your opponent run to play the ball. This is a good strategy if you know you are in better condition than your opponent.

Finally, remember that all ceiling shots travel a great distance, which can cause many errors. Having total control on a ball that is traveling so far is difficult. You should always be thinking about how to use a ceiling shot as an offensive shot and as a defensive shot. This frame of mind is important in successfully using ceiling shots.

Key Elements for the Ceiling Shot

- When using ceiling shots, think both offensively and defensively.

- You need accuracy in placing your ceiling shots into a back corner, but power is also important in reaching the target.

- Use the ceiling shot when you are in trouble because it gives you the best chance of recovery.

- Don't use the ceiling shot when a more offensive shot can be played.

- Hit the ceiling shot at the proper angle to the ceiling and front wall so that the ball does not hit a side wall on its way to a back corner.

- Sometimes ceiling balls seem to be boring. However, the ceiling game is important; take time to practice and perfect it.

Taking Your Game to Its Highest Level   *Woody Clouse*

When hitting a ceiling ball, it should be for offensive reasons, not defensive reasons.

- A ceiling ball will always give you center-court position.

- A ceiling ball will always force your opponent to hit the ball from behind you.

- Whenever you are off balance and in a defensive position, hitting a ceiling ball will give you an offensive opportunity.

- Although the ceiling ball is many times hit from defensive positions, it should be hit with offensive intentions. This will result in much more productivity.

Drills for the Back-Wall Shot

Toss and Catch Drill—No Racquet

Purpose:
To practice side-hitting position, patience, and the arm swing in back-wall shots.

Directions:
Stand near the back wall, toss the ball underhand and low to the back wall, allow the ball to bounce, swing your arm as if you were hitting, but instead catch the ball (25 repetitions).

Variations:
A.   Toss the ball as described above but catch the ball before it bounces on the floor.

B.   Throw the ball to the front wall, let it bounce and hit the back wall, and swing your arm and catch the ball in the air.

Toss and Hit Drill

Purpose:
To hit backhand and forehand back-wall shots with a controlled setup.

Directions:
Stand near the back wall, throw the ball underhand and low to the back wall, allow it to bounce low, and then hit it to the front wall with kill and passing shots (50 repetitions).

Variations:
A.   Bounce the ball to the back wall off the floor and then play the ball in the air off the back wall to the front wall.

B.   Throw the ball underhand and low to the back wall and play the ball in the air before it bounces.

C.   Toss the ball into back corners and repeat the drills.

D.   Throw the ball to the front wall, allow it to bounce on the floor and hit the back wall, and then play it in the air before it bounces. Use passing, kill, and ceiling shots with both fore-hands and backhands.

Front-Wall, Hit the Back-Wall Drill

Purpose:
To play balls coming off the front wall and hit them toward the back wall to learn speeds and angles of rebounds to obtain good positioning for back-wall shots.

Directions:
Stand in the back of the court, hit the ball to the front wall with a passing shot, allow the ball to bounce-hit the back wall, and then play the ball in the air off the back wall (50 repetitions).

Variation:
Hit higher passing shots and ceiling shots to the front wall, allow the ball to bounce-hit the back wall, and repeat the drill.

Drills for the Volley

Self-Toss Drill

Purpose:
To practice the proper positioning and hitting techniques for the volley.

Directions:
Stand between the service lines in a side position, toss the ball low using an underhand toss, and volley the ball to the front wall with passing and kill shots (50 repetitions).

Variations:
A. Begin in the ready position and toss and hit different passing and kill shots off your volley.

B. Begin in the ready position and hit volley ceiling shots.

C. Use backhands as well as forehands in all the drills.

Front-Wall Toss and Volley Drill

Purpose:
To volley a ball coming directly off the front wall.

Directions:
Stand between the service lines facing a side wall, throw the ball underhand to the front wall so that it rebounds into the air, and volley it to the front wall using both forehands and backhands (50 repetitions).

Variations:
A. Begin this drill in the ready position, toss the ball to the front wall, and volley the ball.

B. Stand in the service zone, throw the ball into a front corner, and play the ball in the air with a volley.

Alternate Bounce and Volley Drill

Purpose:
To practice volleying and getting into position in time.

Directions:
Stand in center court and hit the ball to the front wall, allow it to bounce, hit it again to the front wall, and then hit a volley shot; continue rally, alternating volleys and bounce shots (30 repetitions).

Variations:
A. Stand in center court and alternate bounce and volley shots into a front corner.

B. Volley the ball to the front wall and continue to rally using only volley shots; do not allow the ball to bounce.

C. Hit continuous volley shots into the corners and the ceiling.

Drills for the Ceiling Shot

Throw-the-Ceiling Drill

Purpose:
To help the player better understand the flight patterns and power supply needed for overhand ceiling and reverse ceiling shots.

Directions:
Stand in the rear of the court and throw the ball overhand to the ceiling so that it rebounds into a back corner (20 repetitions).

Variation:

Stand farther forward in the court; throw the ball overhand and upward to the front wall so that it rebounds to the ceiling and then lands in a back corner (reverse ceiling).

Drop and Hit Drill

Purpose:
To practice underhand ceiling shots with both the forehand and backhand.

Directions:

Stand in the back of the court, drop the ball waist high, and hit underhand ceiling shots (50 repetitions).

Variations:

A. Toss the ball up high, let it bounce, and hit overhand ceiling shots.

B. Toss the ball high to a side wall, allow it to bounce, and hit either underhand or overhand ceiling shots.

C. Toss the ball high to the back wall, allow it to bounce, and hit either underhand or overhand ceiling shots.

D. Toss the ball high to the front wall, allow it to bounce, and hit either underhand or overhand ceiling shots.

Lob and Ceiling Drill

Purpose:

To play a ceiling shot either underhand or overhand off a high lob shot.

Directions:

Stand deep in the court, bounce the ball, hit a slow, high lob to the front wall (it must be an easy hit), allow the ball to bounce, and hit a ceiling shot to the front wall (20 repetitions).

Variation:

Using the same drill, continue to return the ball to the front wall with a series of ceiling shots in a rally.

Chapter 8

Serving

Photo by Jim Warner—KILLSHOT magazine

Y ou are in control of your racquetball destiny when you are serving because the serve is the only shot that you initiate and control. You position yourself in the service area; you drop the ball; you choose the type of serve; and you decide on service placement. Moreover, the only time you can score points is when you are serving. You must develop an effective serve to score and win.

The serve is an offensive weapon. Planning strategy before you serve is crucial. You must choose the serve and service strategies that will keep your opponent off balance. You control delivery and placement of the shot; your opponent must react. Is the ball moving high or low? Is it hard bouncing or a glancing shot? The decision and the advantage belong to the server.

The server also has an important position advantage. You stand about 16 or 17 feet from the front wall when you serve. If you are serving effectively, your opponent returns the ball from a position approximately 39 feet from the front wall. This distance factor alone gives the server a tremendous advantage over the receiver. In addition, once you have served, you can quickly slide into the center-court area; your opponent must not only return service but also attempt to move you out of center court.

WHERE TO STAND

No two players hit the serve in exactly the same manner, but a number of basic characteristics are common among all successful servers. First, your position in the service zone is important. The best spot is near the center of the service zone with your back foot or both feet on the short line (see Figure 8.1). This position gives you certain advantages. You can quickly reach center-court position. By positioning yourself at the extreme back edge of the service zone, you give yourself enough room to step and slide forward through the serve and still legally remain in the service zone. (The rule for service is that you may be on or touch either service line during service, but you may not cross either line.) You cannot hit a serve with maximum power unless you allow yourself enough room for proper striding, and the short-line position gives you that space. Beginning deep in the service area is especially important for the tall, long-legged player who might footfault forward during a long stride.

BALL DELIVERY

The next aspect of the serve is delivering the ball to initiate the serving action. The rulebook states that you may have one bounce of the ball on each service. Should you drop, toss, or bounce the ball? Making the correct decision is a critical part of service success, yet the question is overlooked by many players. Your decision depends on the type of serve you plan to use, and it dictates your hand position: If your hand is palm down, you will bounce or drop the ball; if it is palm up, you will drop or toss the ball.

Let's consider the perfect toss. The ball should have relatively little spin, and the height of the toss and release depends on the type of serve you wish to hit, how hard, how soft, your target area, and so forth. (Beginners should use a high toss to allow more time for their swing.) Racquet-ball contact should occur at knee level or below on all power serves. Toss the ball slightly in front of you so that you will make contact near the lead foot as you are striding forward. The ball should bounce almost straight up from the floor with little forward or backward momentum. You should hit the ball at the point where it is nearly stationary at the top of this bounce as shown in Figure 8.2. If the ball is moving up or down, it presents a moving target that is more difficult to hit and control; at the top of the bounce, however, the ball is nearly stationary and allows you to hit a more effective serve.

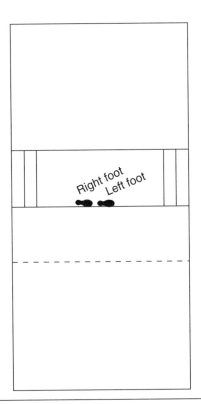

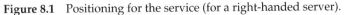

Figure 8.1   Positioning for the service (for a right-handed server).

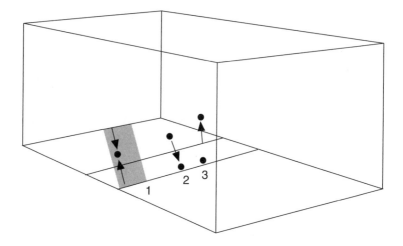

Figure 8.2 Hit a stationary ball, not a moving ball. Ball 1 has reached its peak and is stationary, whereas ball 2 has already begun dropping, and ball 3 is still rising.

Palm-Up Tosses

The best overall technique is a slight toss with the ball held palm up. This allows maximum control of the ball, a soft release, and ample time to execute your backswing. Your hand cradles the ball and prevents it from accidentally falling, which sometimes occurs when holding the ball palm down. Hold the ball on your fingers with your thumb on top of the ball and toss it up gently. Remember that the higher the toss, the more time you have to prepare for your shot. A low toss, however, can help you place the ball lower on the front wall. In any case, do not allow the ball to roll off your fingertips because this gives the ball forward movement with backspin and makes effective racquet-ball contact more difficult.

Palm-Down Tosses

Use the palm-down technique either to drop or to bounce the ball. The grip is the same as for palm up except that the thumb is facing the floor. The drop from this hand position is fairly effective. The only problem is that if you are not careful you may drop the ball before you are ready. Dropping or bouncing the ball with your palm down allows you to add more speed during this portion of your serve. The ball travels a shorter distance or faster than with the toss, so you—

and your opponent—must react more quickly. Of course, you sacrifice a certain amount of preparation time and control when you use the palm-down drop or bounce. You should practice a variety of ball delivery techniques for the serve. Try the different techniques and keep in mind that the palm-up drop is best for the most accurate delivery. You need to find your own comfort zone in ball delivery.

SERVING MOTION MECHANICS

Remember, your basic starting position is near the rear center of the service zone with both feet on the short line. Woody is in the correct position for a left-handed player in Figure 8.3. For the right-handed server, both feet should be pointing toward the forehand side wall and be lined up with each other, heel to toe, with the left foot closest to the side wall.

This position also helps to give a natural legal camouflage to your serve because your body is spread out as you hit the serve, which

Figure 8.3   The correct serve position for a left-handed player.

makes it more difficult for your opponent to watch the ball. In addition, this position gives you several choices on how to begin your stepping approach.

One-Step and Two-Step Approaches

The first footwork technique is the one-step approach. Start in the ready-to-serve position, with the feet parallel to each other, and step forward with the front foot in a power stride. The second technique is a two-step approach beginning with the back foot (right foot for right-handed players, left foot for lefties). Take a short, jabbing crossover step toward the front wall and then step forward with the opposite foot in a longer power stride. Woody, a lefty, in Figure 8.4 has just completed the short jab crossover step.

Another technique in the two-step serve for the right-handed server is to take the right foot (back foot) and swing it forward around your left foot and toward the forehand side wall. The swinging right

Figure 8.4 Woody makes his crossover step for a two-step service approach.

foot is then brought into the service area toward the front wall and placed down. Next the left foot steps toward the front service line. Woody demonstrates this swinging leg technique for lefties in Figure 8.5. This swinging leg two-step approach builds good momentum into your serve. The two-step service approach has a couple of power advantages over the one-step method. By beginning with the back foot first, you open your upper body more toward the back wall so that you are building greater upper-body rotation into the service motion. You are also building up more body momentum by taking two steps instead of one. Both of these elements contribute to a more powerful stroke. But because an extra step is being taken, the skill is more difficult to execute and the added power is hard to control. Numerous variations of these two service approaches are possible, and your foot movements will vary somewhat according to the type of serve you use. In all cases, however, your step is the means of transferring your body weight from the back foot to the front foot, which pulls your upper body around to obtain power.

Figure 8.5   Woody demonstrates the swinging leg version of the two-step service approach.

Racquet Swing

Your racquet swing, especially the backswing, is an important part of a successful serve. Bring your racquet back behind your body as far as you can while still feeling comfortable. Note Woody's backswing in Figure 8.6. Hold your racquet high and extend your elbow as high as comfortably possible. Your wrist should be hyperextended (laid back), and your racquet should be pointing toward the side wall. Your arm should bend naturally at the elbow. This serving backswing position gives you the maximum possible range of service motion. A variety of service backswings are used. But the backswing mechanics we are describing provide the greatest racquet momentum and thus the greatest force. Even though we are stressing power techniques, you must remember that control and placement of your serve is also important. Do not sacrifice control for power.

Your forward swing should be a natural arm swing with the arm being pulled around by the body and shoulders. The swing originates from the high backswing position to a low racquet-ball contact

Figure 8.6   Woody's backswing gives him the maximum range of service motion.

position. Your arm should be partially bent and your elbow should slightly lead the racquet handle. Immediately before impact, your arm should be fully extended, and your racquet head should be pointing to the side wall. You should keep the racquet head parallel to the floor to avoid opening the racquet face, which results in hitting serves high on the front wall.

You should have a natural elbow lead during the swing. This enables you to build more speed into your forearm movement and to impart more speed to the ball. Don't overexaggerate this motion, however, because leading excessively can cause both improper hitting technique and elbow injury. Figure 8.7a shows the beginning of the forward swing.

Ball and Racquet Impact

Racquet-ball impact should be made opposite your front leg at the end of your forward stride, slightly in front of the instep. Your wrist action at impact should be the same flexion-rotation as in all power strokes. Your back leg should partially extend, and your upper body should be rotating so that your arm-and-shoulder action contributes maximum force in the serve (see Figure 8.7b). This movement pattern uses the body as a unit and pulls your racquet around with good force. Keep your head low and watch the ball as Woody is doing in Figure 8.7b. Beginners should watch the ball until impact is made. Advanced players have better hand-eye coordination and might look away from the ball earlier to determine more rapidly their receiver's reaction. Your body should be in a low position with a slightly flexed waist throughout the service delivery.

Follow-Through

The follow-through is another important aspect of service mechanics. It should be natural and should follow your normal range of motion. Do not try to stop the follow-through before it reaches its natural limit. Your follow-through can be high or low depending on the type and power of the stroke. As a rule, a high follow-through is used on lob serves and other high serves. A low follow-through is natural on most power serves since your body is pulling the racquet around. Woody's follow-through in Figure 8.7c is classic. High or low, a full, natural follow-through is essential. You must incorporate

Figure 8.7 Here, Woody demonstrates a well-executed serving motion. From his backswing (see Figure 8.6) he swings down toward the contact point letting his elbow slightly lead his racquet head (a), makes contact (b), and follows through (c).

all the elements of hitting mechanics to serve with power and accuracy—stepping, shifting of body weight, wrist action, leg extension, arm action, shoulder action, and upper body rotation—and the proper follow-through is the culmination of these basic elements.

TYPES OF SERVES

As you read about serves, you will see references to drive serves, Z serves, half-lob serves, lob serves, crosscourt serves, power serves, lob Z serves, garbage serves, and many more. All of these serves are derived from three forms: the drive serve, the Z serve, and the lob serve. Over the years, the three basic serves have been modified significantly, and now many servers hit combination serves that incorporate elements of two, and sometimes all three, of the basic serves. Possessing a variety of basic serves and service variations is important for keeping your opponent off balance.

Drive Serve

The drive serve is one of racquetball's most common and powerful shots. To hit it with maximum force, you must use all the elements in the power supply. Your lead shoulder should be level, your wrist hyperextended (cocked back), and the butt of your racquet pointed toward the front wall. Your lead foot should be parallel or at a slight angle to the front wall. The slight angle or parallel foot helps you get maximum upper-body rotation into the serve.

You should drop the ball low and hit it at knee level or lower, approximately opposite the instep of your lead foot. You should begin at the short line and move forward in the service zone as racquet-ball contact is made. Beginners through advanced-level players can hit drive serves from slightly left of center service court against right-handed opponents and from slightly right of center service court against left-handed opponents. At the highest level of play, most individuals serve from near the center of the service zone. This positioning allows you to give many serves the same look and gives you equal distance for serve placement to either side of the court. This position also places you close to center court. Speed and power are important aspects of the drive serve, and the shorter the distance the ball travels, the greater the speed it will maintain. Therefore, contacting the ball at the front of the service zone and hitting it relatively straight to the front wall makes it travel the shortest distance and gives the receiver the least time to react to the ball.

The perfect drive serve is hit very hard and barely clears the short service line. You should not hit the ball any deeper than five feet past the short service line. Direct the ball toward a back corner as in Figure 8.8; it should either bounce twice or more before reaching the corner or die in a back corner after one bounce. The drive serve is designed to win the point outright or to make your opponent reach and dig for the ball. An effective drive serve must have both accuracy and velocity.

You should not hit down or up on the drive serve as you put it into play. Drop the ball at the proper height to hit the ball straight toward

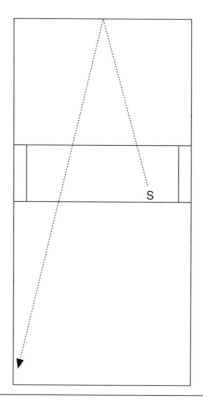

Figure 8.8   The flight path of the drive serve.

the front wall. A downward or upward hit changes the rebounding action of the ball on the first bounce and may give a better opportunity to return service.

Ball Spin

Most players do not attempt to put any type of spin on drive serves or other types of serves. However, a little natural backspin can make the drive serve more effective because backspin makes the ball rebound quicker off the front wall and stay closer to the floor after it takes its first bounce. On the other hand, topspin is a liability. A ball hit with topspin grabs the front wall longer and has a higher initial bounce off the floor, which gives the receiver a better chance of returning the serve.

Even though some backspin can be a useful variation, a flat ball, which has little or no spin, is the most effective for the drive serve. Remember that you must angle the racquet face slightly to impart spin on the ball, and this always involves some loss of power on the shot. A flat ball has all the power directly behind the ball, thus giving you maximum speed.

Drive Serve Variations

If you do not possess the ability to hit the ball with offensive force, you should consider variations of the drive serve. You can vary the drive serve by moving to different spots within the service zone and by hitting the ball at different speeds. If you move toward the sides of the service zone, the drive serve is hit at more of an angle and is very similar to a crosscourt passing shot (see Figure 8.9). This angled or crosscourt drive serve allows your opponent more time to get to the ball because it travels a greater distance and has a slower speed than the basic drive serve. You may also hit the drive serve slower

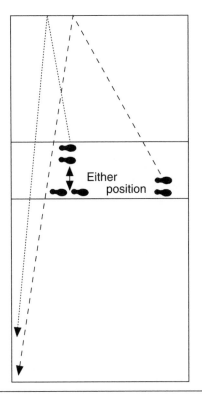

Figure 8.9   The wide deep drive serve compared with the straight forward serve. Notice the greater distance the ball travels in the wide serve as compared with the straight forward serve.

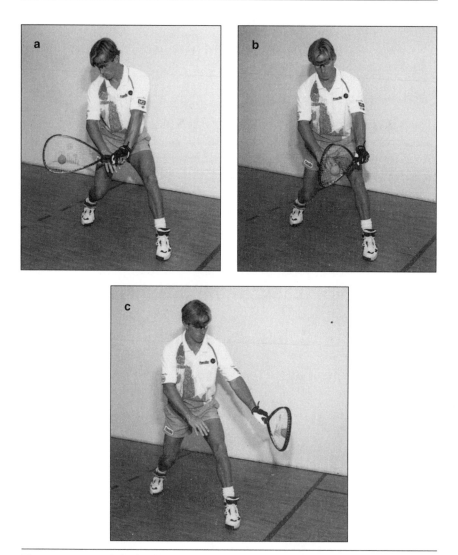

Figure 8.10 For lefty backhands, contacting the ball slightly behind the body gets a right angled shot (a); contacting the ball opposite the front hip gives you a straight shot (b); and ball contact in front of your body gives you a left angled shot (c).

and strive for accuracy by placing the ball at three-quarter or half-speed into the back corners. In addition, you can achieve different angles on your serve by changing the position of racquet-ball contact. For a right-handed server a ball can be angled right by contacting it slightly behind your body midline, and the serve can be angled left by playing the ball slightly in front of your body midline. Figure 8.10 shows the different racquet-ball contacts of a lefty changing the angle of his shot.

Drive Serve Placement

When you hit your serve, you want to put the ball on the front wall so that it is launched on a flight path that dies in one of the back corners. The ball should never rebound out of a back corner; if it does, your opponent gets a clear hit on the ball. On the drive serve, the ball should not hit a side wall because this causes the ball to go into center court and sets up the receiver for an offensive shot. Figure 8.11 shows the correct placement into the corners for drive serves.

A practice method helpful for beginners and intermediate-level players for all types of serves, particularly for the drive serve, uses targets on the front wall. The targets indicate where the ball should

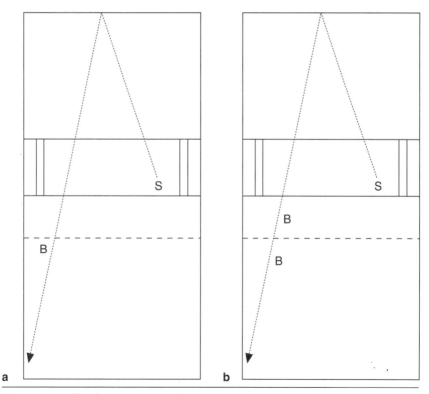

Figure 8.11 The drive serve may bounce once and die in the corner (a) or it may take two quick bounces to reach the corner (b).

Figure 8.12 X marks the spot: Use targets to help you drill your serve placement.

land on the front wall so that it rebounds into the court at exactly the right place (see Figure 8.12). You may also use Xs in the service area so that you consistently serve to the same target from the same spot to get identical ball rebounding angles.

Crotch Drive Serves

Crotch serves, which hit the junction of the side wall and floor beyond the short line, are excellent drive serves because the ball either bounces erratically after hitting the crotch or rolls out on the floor. The server scores an ace or has a setup on the returned ball. The problem with a crotch serve is that the target area is very small, and consistently hitting the crotch is very difficult. If you hit the serve a little too high, the ball hits the side wall and rebounds to center court and the receiver gets advantageous position. However, sometimes the server can get in a groove and hit a succession of crotch serves and win many points. Drive the crotch serve mainly to the backhand corner of the receiver because most players, excluding touring pros, are weak in the backhand. This is a good strategy for all serves, especially the hard-hit drive serve.

To reduce the effectiveness of the drive serve and to help eliminate screens, a drive zone service area has been created. Within the service zone there are two lines running parallel to the doubles service box line three feet from each side wall. You may not touch or cross this line with the ball delivery, with the foot, or during racquet-ball contact on a drive serve on the side of the court where you are standing. This drive zone does not apply to crosscourt drives or any other serve.

Lob Serves

The lob serve is totally different from other serves because touch, rather than power, is the key to success. However, like all serves, proper angles and execution are important. The lob serve is more of a push serving action when hit overhand. You should use very little wrist-snap, your hitting-arm movement should originate from the shoulder, and your hitting arm should remain fairly straight. For the underhand lob serve, drop your racquet head slightly and swing up on the ball with a stiff wrist to give it the necessary upward trajectory. Figure 8.13 shows Woody correctly "pushing" the underhand lob (a) and incorrectly using the wrist (b).

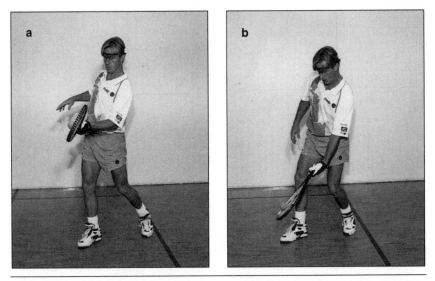

Figure 8.13 Use a firm wrist for the lob serve and drop your racquet head slightly (a). Do not go with a weak wrist or drop your head at an extreme angle (b).

Because the lob serve is a touch shot, the power sources are not as important as in the drive serve. Although a variety of lob serves can be played, the two basic lob serves are the half-lob and the high lob. The purpose of the lob serve is to hit the ball high on the front wall and have it end up in one of the back corners at about shoulder height of the receiver, forcing a ceiling return. Accuracy of ball delivery for the overhand lob can be a problem because you are bouncing or tossing the ball a great distance with your nondominant hand. Spend time practicing your toss or bounce for lob serves. The underhand lob serve toss is much easier to control than the overhand lob serve toss. But the ball on the underhand lob serve must go through a greater distance than on the overhand lob serve and therefore there is a greater chance for error using the underhand technique.

Half-Lob Serve

The half-lob is probably the easiest and most practical serve in racquetball. The ball travels a relatively short distance and is hit at a slow speed, and thus it is an easy mechanical skill. You can use the half-lob as a change of pace, as a second serve, and as an offensive first serve. It makes your opponent contend with a chest-to shoulder-high return. The five-foot receiving line has helped make the half-lob an excellent choice of serves. Because the receiver cannot be in or play

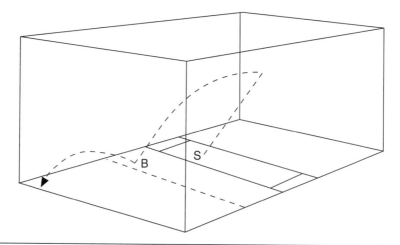

Figure 8.14 The correct landing spots for the half-lob serve. The serve hits 10 to 13 feet high on the front wall, bounces on the floor in the safety zone, and dies in the back corner.

a ball in the safety zone (the five-foot area between receiving line and short line), the half-lob cannot easily be picked off with a volley. As with most of your serves, the ball should end up deep in the back corners (see Figure 8.14). The half-lob is most effective in the backhand corner since your opponent must hit a high backhand shot on the service return. A high backhand service return will usually be a ceiling shot because hitting kills and passing shots off a high backhand service return is difficult for most players. If your opponent attempts to kill or pass, he or she will probably make an error.

Your body position for the half-lob should be the same as for all serves. Your service area location should be slightly off center toward your opponent's backhand side. The ball can take one of two paths: You can angle it slightly toward the backhand corner or hit it almost parallel to the backhand side wall. We recommend the parallel half-lob because it hugs the side wall and makes a difficult return. In either case, the ball should not hit the side wall because this puts it into the center-court area. The tendency to hit the side wall is greater with the parallel half-lob than with the slightly angled half-lob.

Hit the ball 10 to 13 feet high on the front wall. It should gently rebound into the safety zone at the dotted line and end up in a back corner at shoulder height of your opponent. Remember to use a stiff wrist. The stroke should come from your shoulder, and the elbow on the hitting arm should be slightly bent. This type of swing gives you better control on the ball. There is no deception when you are serving lob serves so it is important to be accurate with both your toss and your service mechanics.

High Lob Serve

Like the half-lob serve, the key factors in successfully using the high lob serve are touch and placement. Hit the high lob serve around 16 to 18 feet high on the front wall. The ball should rebound in the five-foot safety zone, or close to it, and end up in one of the back corners (see Figure 8.15). The high lob serve makes the service receiver contend with a ball coming almost straight down, and this downward trajectory can cause errors in the service return. On the negative side, the high lob serve goes so high that it gives the receiver sufficient time to move into position to play the ball.

You can use the high lob serve as a change-of-pace serve or as a high offensive serve to both the backhand and forehand corners of your opponent. Your stroking action is similar to that of the half-lob

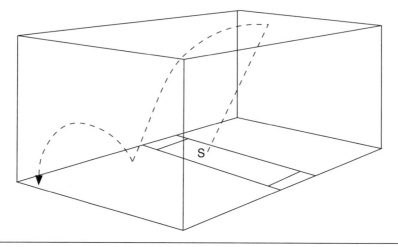

Figure 8.15   The high lob serve.

serve. Again, touch and control are important. The ball should neither rebound out from the back wall nor deflect off the side wall. If either of these situations occur, you will be giving the receiver a setup. You should stand either along the backhand side wall or slightly to the backhand side of center service court. You can hit the high lob at a slight angle to the front wall or parallel to the side wall. Be aware that the receiver has plenty of time to react to a high lob serve. He or she may move forward, short of the receiving line, and play the high lob in the air as a volley. On all down-the-wall lob serves, try to keep the ball in a five-foot wide alley along the side wall. This technique gives you some margin for error and should stop most lob serves from hitting the side wall and becoming setups. A lob serve that glances off the side wall near the back corner and hugs the back wall can be an effective weapon.

Z Serve

The last of the three basic serves is the Z serve. This is one of the best serves in racquetball because you can make slight errors on the shot and still come out with an effective serve. The Z serve obtains its name from the Z path that the ball follows. When properly executed, the Z can create some real problems for the receiver in both the backhand and forehand corners. The stroking pattern is similar to that of the drive serve except that the server is angling the ball into a front corner. There are many variations of the Z serve concerning where the server stands, how hard to hit the ball, how high to hit the ball, and exactly what the ball should do in the back corner.

Placement

With the Z serve, the ball should end up in the back corner of the side from which you serve. The typical Z serve hits the front wall about four to six feet high and about one foot from the side wall opposite your serving position. After hitting the front wall and the side wall, the ball cuts across court on a diagonal, bounces on the floor within the five-foot safety area, hits the side wall near your service position, and either angles toward the back wall or comes off the side wall close to and parallel to the back wall.

Power and Angles

Ball speed and front-wall angle determine whether the ball ends up parallel to the back wall or angled toward the back wall. The closer to the corner you hit the ball, the more spin the ball will have and the more likely it will rebound parallel to the back wall. Hitting the front wall farther from the corner puts less spin on the ball and sends it toward the back wall at an angle. You must hit the Z serve with enough power. (See Figure 8.16 for the ball flight pattern in hard hit Z serves.) Hitting with too little power also causes the ball to angle toward the back wall rather than coming off the side wall parallel to the back wall. Let's discuss some of the more common problems associated with the Z serve. A Z serve to the backhand corner that hits the backhand side wall more than a few feet from the back wall causes the ball to bounce to the middle of the court. This means you are hitting the front wall too close to the side wall and you may be hitting with too much power. Hit the Z serve with a little less power and a little farther from the front corner.

If your Z serve is hitting the back wall before it hits the backhand side wall, you are hitting the front wall too far from the side wall. This allows your opponent an easy return.

The Z serve should hit the floor within the five-foot safety zone behind the short line. If your serve is landing outside the five-foot safety zone, you are probably hitting too hard for the height of the shot. You can correct the problem by hitting with less power. Where

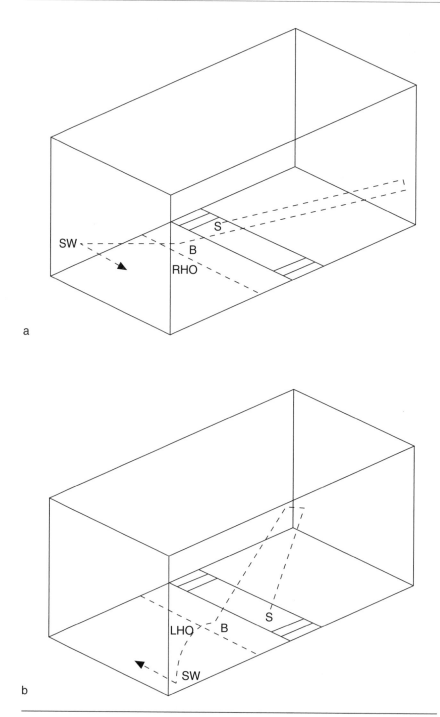

Figure 8.16   The ball path of an effective Z serve for playing against a right-handed opponent (a) and against a left-handed opponent (b).

the ball hits the floor on the Z serve is very important. The farther behind the five-foot receiving line it lands, the easier it is for the receiver to cut off the ball while it is in the air. Also, many Z serves that hit the floor behind the safety zone come off the back wall too high and result in a setup.

Positioning

Disagreement exists concerning service area positioning for hitting the Z serve. Some argue that all serves should be hit from the same spot—to use deception—and that the best spot is the center of the service zone. This places the server close to center-court position. However, hitting the Z serve from the center of the service zone requires you to hit the ball much closer to the side-wall crotch than when you are to one side of the service box. Using center position makes accuracy critical in the success of the Z serve. If the shot is only slightly off target, you might hit the side wall first. Standing to one side of the service box increases target size, increases the front-wall angles of your serve, changes the spin on the ball, and makes the receiver's job more difficult. Figure 8.17 shows you a variety of positions for the Z serve and Figure 8.18 shows the different angles from some of the different positions.

Variations of the Z Serve

Variations of the standard Z serve include the low-power Z, the high-lob Z, and the garbage Z. The low-power Z should hit about three feet high on the front wall and is played from the backhand side of the service zone. Executed properly, the low-power Z rebounds parallel with and close to the back wall. Use somewhat more power than with the standard Z.

You must hit the high-lob Z much softer than either the low-power Z or the standard Z serve. The ball should hit the front wall 15 to 17 feet high within 2 feet of the side wall. The high-lob Z should take such a high bounce into the backhand corner that the receiver must play the ball directly out of the corner. The receiver should try to volley the lob Z before it bounces.

Hit the garbage Z 10 feet high on the front wall. The ball should follow basically the same pattern of flight as the lob Z. This serve gives your opponent a little less time to react to the ball and imparts slightly different spin and angles on the ball than the other Z serves (see Figure 8.19). Therefore, you can use the garbage Z as an effective change-of-pace serve.

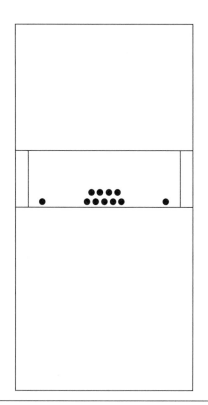

Figure 8.17   The Z serve positions.

Combination-Variation Serves

The basics of most sports skills seem to be modified almost constantly, and racquetball serves are no exception. Many effective serves are not true Zs, lobs, or drives but use changes in speed, angle, placement, and height. You can combine or vary any of the three basic serves. Most racquetball players hit serves that are slightly different from the three basic serves. Players often find combinations or var-iations that give their serves greater consistency and offensive power.

Common variations include three-quarter drive serves, half-drive serves, high side-wall drives, low side-wall drives, crosscourt serves, reverse crosscourt serves, garbage serves, lob drive serves, and wallpaper serves. You can hit underhand serves, sidearm serves, overhand serves, serves from the center service zone, and serves from other spots in the service zone. As Figure 8.20 suggests, you can

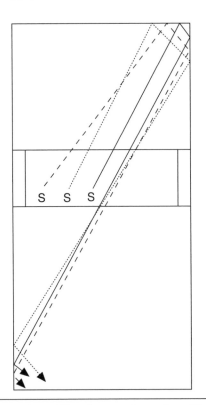

Figure 8.18 The Z server's position changes the angles of the serve, but the ball still ends in the back corner or bouncing parallel to the back wall.

use soft lobs, soft drives, and soft Zs, or hard lobs, hard drives, and hard Zs. You can hit high or low lobs, drives, and Zs. Of course, we shouldn't forget right-handed serves, left-handed serves, backhand serves, and forehand serves.

The important concept in selecting a serve is to find one that you are comfortable with and that helps you win points. Be creative and invent a combination-variation serve to fit your needs.

SERVICE STRATEGY

You can and should use many strategies to increase your chances of hitting service winners. This portion of the chapter will detail some of the most effective strategies. First, let's review the basics of service

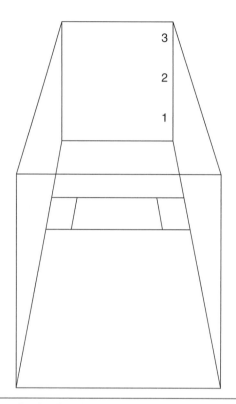

Figure 8.19 Targets for the three basic Z serves: 1. standard Z; 2. garbage Z; 3. lob Z.

strategy. These points may seem obvious, yet are often overlooked. Keep these principles foremost in your mind each time you line up to serve.

- **Exploit Weaknesses.** Identify your opponent's weakness and use the serves that best exploit that weakness. If you are not sure which serve to use, try a variety of serves to pinpoint the receiver's weakness. Once you find the chink in the armor, bang away at it.

- **Concentrate.** Don't just go into the service zone and flail away. Have a plan for the serve *and* for the point. Know exactly what serve you will hit and where it will go. You must also concentrate on the ball and on the mechanics of your serve. Visualize the serve before you hit it.

- **Play Percentages.** Once you have hit a successful serve, play both high and low percentage shots throughout the point. Remem-

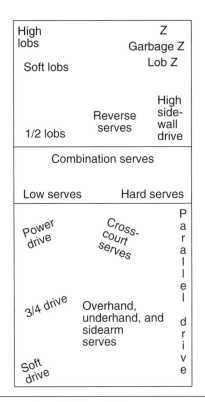

Figure 8.20 The many and varied faces of the serve.

ber that you cannot lose a point when serving; the worst you can do is to lose the serve. So be aggressive. When you're on serve, go for the put-away shots *and* mix in a few shots that may have a lower chance of success. Cover any balls that you have even a hair's chance of hitting. You may win a difficult point.

Disguise and Deception

Deception is a key factor in serving. You deceive your opponent by making all your serves look alike. Hit most of your serves from the same position in the service court, and make the mechanics look the same so your opponent is never sure what is coming until the ball is off the wall.

Of course, you can, at times, move to a new service location or change your mechanics. This broadcasts that another type of serve is

Key Elements for Service Success

- For most serves, position yourself near the center back of the service zone because this places you closest to the center-court area. However, this center service positioning does not afford the best angles.

- Practice your ball delivery technique; it is critical to the success of your serve.

- Most serves should land in a back corner; this forces the receiver to contend with the side and back walls and puts him or her as far from the front wall as possible.

- Accuracy is more important in serving than power, yet ultimately you would like to hit many serves with both accuracy and power.

- As a beginner, adopt one serve that you like and use it about 70 to 80 percent of the time; pick another serve and use it about 15 to 20 percent of the time; try other serves occasionally for a change of pace.

- As you advance in skill you should have a repertoire of six or seven serves that are effective for you.

Taking Your Game to Its Highest Level   *Woody Clouse*

Drive Serves
Each drive serve should be hit with the intent to ace your opponent.

- Never assume that your opponent is going to hit a poor return shot.

- Always keep low through your serving motion.

- Mix up your drive serves.

- Know the spot on the front wall you need to hit to produce the angle you desire.

- Don't always stand in the center of the service box. Occasionally serve from the sides of the service box to get better angles.

- Visualize your serve being successful before you hit.

Lob Serves

Remember, the lob serve can be just as powerful and effective as the drive serve.

- Hit lob serves with the intent to produce a setup for your next shot.
- Always be ready if your opponent cuts off your lob serve.
- Force your opponent to dig your serve out of a corner.

Z Serves

The Z serve is the best way to stay aggressive when your drive serves aren't working.

- Hit the Z serve deep into the corner so your opponent can't cut off the ball.
- Hit the Z serve high, about shoulder height, so your opponent has to hit down on it.
- When you're hitting a Z serve low, the intent should be to deceive your opponent and catch him or her off balance.

coming, and you should work this to your advantage. If you hit two or three nicely disguised scoring serves from your basic position and then you force a new serve on your opponent, you're saying, "I'm so confident I can beat you that I'm going to use something other than my bread-and-butter serves. And what's more, I'm going to *show* you what's coming." This psychological edge, backed up by excellent execution, can make you a dominating server. In addition, changing service technique lets you command the flow of play and unbalances the receiver. Consider serving one or two new serves, returning to your basic serving position and mechanics, and then repeating and varying the sequence.

All of your serves can be disguised in some way; however, the most important serves to disguise are the low drive and low Z serves. Because these are fast serves, cutting your opponent's reaction time, even for a fraction of a second, is definitely advantageous. The lob, half-lob, and lob Z serves can be partially disguised, but these are slower serves and take longer to reach the receiver, so deception is not as important. To disguise a serve well, consider body position, ball position, feet position, shoulder position, racquet position, and screen rules.

Body Position

Remember to follow the rules for the basic hitting position described in chapter 5. For the low, hard serves your body should be in a semicrouched, low position, and for high, softer serves you can be more upright. Remember, the goal is to make all serves look the same until the ball is contacted. In addition, your body itself can help to disguise the ball. Depending upon your position in the service court, the angle at which you hit your serve, and the receiver's position, your body can act somewhat as a legal screen on the ball. You can position yourself to slightly obstruct your opponent's view of the ball by lining yourself up with the middle of your opponent and the point of the service ball's contact on the front wall.

Feet Position and Stride

Your feet positioning can also help to disguise your serve. For example, if you and your opponent are right-handed, line up with your left foot in line with the receiver's left foot, *after* she or he moves into position (see Figure 8.21). This position allows you legally to block your opponent's view of the ball for a split second. The length of your stride into the ball also helps in disguising your various serves. All else being equal, the length of the stride into the ball determines where your racquet contacts the ball in relation to your body alignment. By varying your stride by four to six inches, you can alter your serve without the receiver seeing it.

Racquet Position

The racquet position relative to your body and the relationship between the racquet face and ball contact will also help you change your serve. Dropping the head, angling the face (either more open or more closed), and contacting the ball a little in front of or behind your body provide a variety of ways to change and disguise your serve. Both angles and ball flight patterns are changed by adjusting racquet face or head position, but remember to keep your shoulder positioning consistent. The point of ball-racquet contact is the best way to deceive your opponent.

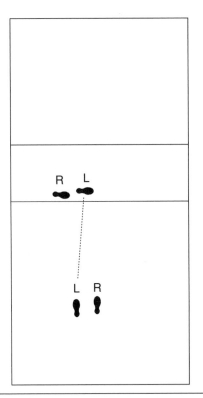

Figure 8.21 Disguising the serve with the server's left foot in line with the receiver's left foot.

Ball Delivery

Another important aspect of service disguise is your delivery. If you deliver the ball close to or slightly in front of your body, the receiver's view will be obstructed. Delivering the ball wide of your body gives the receiver a better view of racquet-ball contact, which allows him or her to anticipate more easily your serve. Proper body and shoulder alignment and hitting the ball at arm's length gives you the most mechanically efficient serve.

Screen Rules

Disguising your serves is important, but the camouflaging must conform to the rules of the game. The screen serve rule defines a screen ball as one that passes so close to the server that the view of the returning side is obstructed. Most interpreters of the rule use the minimum distance of 18 inches from the body. Any time a ball rebounds in the receiver's area and passes within 18 inches of the server's body, it is a screen ball and a fault serve. Do not try to disguise the serve by obstructing the receiver in violation of the screen serve rule. The methods of service disguise described in this chapter are designed to give the receiver less anticipation time on your serve while allowing you to play within the rules.

Serve to the Back Corners

Most advanced servers employ identical strategies and skill mechanics when putting the ball into play. All servers should strive to hit their serves consistently deep into the back corners of the court. If you can place the serve in the back corners, you can win the point outright with an ace; you can force a weak return from the receiver that you can put away on the ensuing shot; or you can cause the receiver to hit the service return defensively with a ceiling ball. Above all, you do not want your serve to glance off a side wall or to rebound hard off the back wall into the center-court area. This changes the receiver from a defensive player to an offensive player, and the dominating effect of your serve is lost.

The server can exercise a good deal of control over both the type of serve played and the receiver's return and rally. You must consider four factors to achieve both levels of service control. First, you must decide on the type of serve to use based on your strength and offensive style of play. Second, you should choose the serve that takes advantage of the receiver's weaknesses and defensive capabilities. Third, you must select the appropriate spot in the service area from which to serve. Fourth, you must consider the type of return you want your opponent to make.

Serve to the Backhand Strategy

For whatever reason, many players have weaker backhands than forehands. This shouldn't be so, but it is. That's why serving to your opponent's backhand remains an important strategy. When you have not scouted a player, test his or her backhand returns first. Keep the ball deep and in the back corners, camouflage your serves, vary your serves, and change pace with your serves. If you find that the backhand is the weakness, don't hesitate to exploit it in every possible way.

Hit soft serves against a hard hitter, and use fast shots against the slower paced player. If you are playing a receiver who continually goes to the ceiling, utilize low, hard serves that give the opponent the least amount of time to get set up.

Z Serve to Receiver's Backhand

The most advantageous Z serve is mainly to your opponent's backhand corner. This does not mean that you cannot serve an effective Z serve to your opponent's forehand. The basic position for the server against right-handed players is the far left of the service zone and near the front service line. (If you are playing a left-handed hitter, position yourself to the far right of the service zone.) This is the easiest position from which to deliver successful Z serves. One problem, however, is that the position itself may telegraph a Z serve to the receiver. Another problem is that you have placed yourself far from center court. However, because the Z serve takes a fairly long time to reach the back corner, you should have enough time to take center court.

SECOND SERVES

Second serves may soon be a thing of the past. The pro tour has already gone to a one-serve rule to speed game times and to make hard drive serves more risky. (Theoretically, this discourages boom-boom points and makes the game more interesting.) The AARA is experimenting with the one-serve rule in the open division of sanctioned tournaments. So it's possible that all sanctioned tournaments will move to the one-serve rule in the near future. Until then, remember that everybody misses a first serve now and then.

What should you do on your second serve? Remember that you have just as many options for the second serve as you do for the first serve. Also, all of the qualities for successful serving apply equally to the second and first serves. The only real difference between the first and second serve is the added pressure that you must now hit a successful serve or you will become the receiver. Therefore, job number one is to get the ball in play. The next consideration is to keep the second serve offensive.

Here are two simple strategies for second serving:

- **KISS the Second Serve.** KISS (Keep it simple, stupid) is a good rule of thumb. Use a serve that is easy to hit and is at the same time an offensive shot. The lob serve meets both of these criteria. The high lob and the half-lob are quite good as second serves. The hitting mechanics are comparatively simple, and if you place the serve correctly, your opponent will have only defensive returns. You can also try Z serves, slow drives, garbage serves, and others as a second serve. A good technique for practicing second serves—especially when you're out in front in a match—is to hit some of your second serves on first service attempts.

- **Maintain Concentration.** This should be obvious, but many players—even faced with the possibility of losing serve—don't concentrate as intently on the second serve as they do on the first. As with the first serve, think about where you want to place the serve and how you intend to play the point before putting the ball in play.

Finally, occasionally try a few unexpected second serves to keep your opponent off balance. Don't slack off on your second serve; you are still the server and you should still be on the offensive.

RELOCATION AFTER SERVING

Center court is the high rent district of the racquetball court. You want to get there and stay. As shown in Figure 8.22, the center-court position is the oval area behind the short line approximately 15 feet wide and 8 feet to 10 feet deep. Your service strategy must include a technique for taking control of this area after delivering the serve.

Three major relocation errors can occur. First, you might serve and stay in the service zone. This makes you quite vulnerable to any good passing shot even though you are in good position to retrieve kills. If you have an effective offensive serve, you will be faced with few kill returns, so remaining in the service area after serving is obviously not the best position.

A second relocation error is running in a small circular path to get to center court. This takes more time than a straight drop-back and

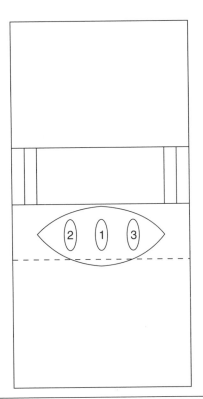

Figure 8.22 Relocate after serving to: 1. center court; 2. left-center court; or 3. right-center court.

Key Elements for Service Strategies

- Keep your second serve simple but use it offensively.
- By using *very slight* changes in ball delivery and the position of feet, you can disguise a variety of serves.
- You may also use your point of racquet-ball contact, service contact with the front wall, and alignment of your body with the receiver to legally screen the ball.
- Exploit your opponent's weaknesses, hit to the backhand, hit your serves into the back corners, vary your serves, and concentrate when you are serving.

thus is not very practical. The circle pattern may be used if you are afraid of being hit by the ball or if you need to give your opponent more hitting area. But neither of these reasons is sound if you are serving effectively because the straight drop-back will give your opponent ample hitting opportunities without hitting you.

Third is retreating too deeply into center court. If you retreat too deeply, you are not set for the next return because it takes quite a bit of time to move out of deep center court, and you would be vulnerable to any hard-driven passing or kill shots. However, the deep position is effective if you know your opponent is going to the ceiling on the return.

To overcome these three basic errors, you must develop and practice proper mechanics for moving to center court immediately following your service. Let's consider this now.

Moving to Center Court

The serving stride is forward, away from center court. So how does one serve and then take center court? The key is learning how to change directions. As you step forward into your serve, allow your back foot to drag a little. This drag action should not impede your power, but it should act as a pivot point to begin moving back into center court after contacting the service ball. Note Woody's back foot in Figure 8.23.

After hitting the serve, you must immediately turn your head to the side of the court where you placed your serve to determine how your opponent will play it. As Woody demonstrates in Figure 8.24, as you turn your head, you simultaneously turn your upper body slightly and begin to step or shuffle backwards into center-court position. *At all times you must have your opponent and the ball in sight.* Move quickly into center court so that you achieve that position before your opponent returns your serve. Be sure to keep your body low, in a semicrouched position, as you move. This enables you to move rapidly and keeps you in the ideal hitting position. If, after serving, you hesitate even a fraction of a second before you begin turning and moving, you will not have time to take center court and to get set before your opponent returns the serve. Figure 8.25 shows Woody in center court still watching the opponent and the ball.

Each player has his or her variations on the technique to move to center court. No matter what technique you employ, it is vitally important to obtain center court quickly while watching your opponent and the ball. Practice this technique as a normal part of practic-

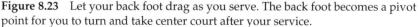

Figure 8.23 Let your back foot drag as you serve. The back foot becomes a pivot point for you to turn and take center court after your service.

ing your serves. Concentrate particularly on gaining center court from the backhand serving spot in the service zone since you will most likely be hitting most of your serves to your opponent's backhand.

Overshading on Relocation

Several circumstances may cause you to slightly shade your drop-back movement toward center court to one side or the other. On the defensive side, you may have made an error on your serve, causing the ball to come out to center court, and you must move to one side to allow your opponent an unobstructed return. You may also overshade for offensive reasons. Overshading can legally cut off some of your opponent's returns. For instance, as shown in Figure 8.26, if you serve into the opponent's backhand corner and you overshade slightly to the backhand side of the court, you can cut off some of the crosscourt passing shot returns by obstructing the angle with your body. You can thus force your opponent to hit down-the-wall or to the ceiling.

Figure 8.24 After serving, turn your head toward the ball to check your opponent's return and begin to shuffle to the center court position.

Figure 8.25 Woody in center court watching for his opponent's return.

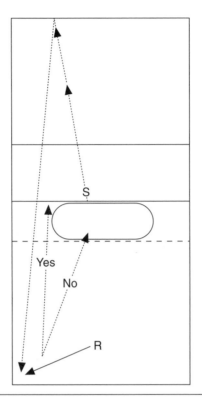

Figure 8.26 Cutting off angles with relocation: by overshading left the server has forced the receiver (R) to hit a ceiling shot or down-the-wall passing shot. Crosscourt passes have been cut off.

Drills for Serves

(About one third of your total practice time.)

Ball Delivery Drill

Purpose:

To practice delivering the ball properly, accurately, and with the right timing.

Directions:

Stand slightly left of the center of the service zone with your feet on the short line; practice dropping the ball consistently low for the drive serve; do not hit the ball (20 repetitions).

Variations:

    A. Repeat the drill delivering the ball for lob serves.

    B. Repeat the drill delivering the ball for Z serves.

    C. After good ball delivery is achieved, repeat the drills and hit the ball.

Serving Drill

Purpose:

To practice serving drive serves to a left-handed opponent.

Directions:

Stand slightly left of the center of the service zone with your feet on the short service line, practice dropping the ball low consistently for the drive serve; do not hit the ball.

Variations:

    A. Repeat the drill by hitting ten lob serves in succession.

    B. Repeat the drill by hitting ten Z serves in succession.

    C. Alter your starting position to the left, right, or forward; repeat the succession drill with each serve.

    D. Vary the drill with different speeds, angles, and heights and hit ten successive serves of each type.

    E. Alternate different serves as well as speeds, angles, and heights and hit ten successive serves.

Target Drill

Purpose:

To provide points of aim and reference points in the service zone.

Directions:

Place three-foot by three-foot targets in various strategic aiming spots on the front wall; attempt to hit the target with your serves so that the serve is effective and offensive (50 repetitions).

Variations:

    A. Place the targets high for lobs, low for drives, and about four to five feet high and in the corner areas for Zs.

    B. Tape reference targets in the service zone so that by always serving from the same spot you improve your service consistency.

Chapter 9

Returning Serve

Photo by Jim Warner—KILLSHOT magazine

*R*eturning serves may be the most difficult skill in racquet-ball because the server has so much control—of both the serve and your return options. Serving is predominantly an offensive strategy. Your strategy in returning service centers on neutralizing the server's control and putting the server on the defensive. In this chapter we'll tell you how to take control by returning service.

THE MECHANICS OF SERVICE RETURNS

Naturally, there is more to hitting effective service returns than sending the ball back to the front wall and hoping the server will be caught off guard. You'll want to anticipate the serve and prepare an aggressive antidote to the service strategy. But the best return strategy won't help if you can't execute. So let's take a look at your ready position, court positioning, and footwork before we discuss shot selection and strategy.

Ready Position

The basic ready position for returning service starts with the feet comfortably apart and in line with the shoulders for a good base of support. As Woody shows in Figure 9.1, your weight is forward on

Figure 9.1   Woody shows the proper form for the return-of-serve position. Note that his weight is on the balls of the feet.

the balls of the feet so that you can easily move in any direction. Your knees are slightly bent, your body is slightly flexed at the waist, and your shoulders are parallel to the front wall while you watch the server and the ball. Your arms are partially bent, and your elbows are fairly close to the body. Because most serves will be to your backhand side, hold the racquet with a backhand grip. Hold the racquet even with the midline of the body at shoulder height. This provides the shortest backswing distance, the quickest return, and the best mechanics for power generation.

Beginners may wish to try the two-handed backhand grip with the nonhitting hand on the throat above the gripping hand. The nonhitting hand can help to turn the racquet when changing grips, which gives more control.

Court Position

Your position in the court should be midway between the side walls and anywhere from four to five feet from the back wall. Here you should be able to retrieve balls as easily from your backhand side as your forehand side. If your backhand is weaker (shame on you), you may wish to overshade slightly to the backhand side to compensate. But against players of even intermediate skill, the slightest overshading or leaning of the body weight to one side is an open invitation for the server to ace you on the opposite side with a good power-drive serve.

You may vary your distance from the back wall slightly. If the server is hitting poor serves for easy setups, you may move forward up to nine feet from the back wall to cut off the ball for a put-away shot. This *up* positioning also creates a psychological edge. You are now taking an *assuming*, or anticipating, position, and sometimes this aggressive strategy takes away part of the server's edge.

Watch the Server

You should be watching the server closely. Pay attention to the server's position in the service zone and try to notice cues that telegraph the upcoming serve. The server's position in the service zone will often tell you what to expect. Many players deliver particular serves from certain locations. If you can anticipate the upcoming serve by the server's positioning, you can get a jump on the ball and thus reduce the effectiveness of the service. Body positioning, ball delivery, and preliminary mechanics may also be cues. For example, if the server left of the center of the service zone drops the ball far from his or her body, the only effective serve is a crosscourt drive.

Footwork

Some receivers like to be moving or bouncing slightly so they can already be in motion to move and react quickly to the serve. The physics principle—that a body already in motion is easier to keep in motion—certainly holds true here. You may bounce slightly, shuffle your feet slightly, or almost run slowly in place. You should always have one foot in contact with the floor so that you are stable and able to push off quickly in any direction.

React to the serve as soon as or before the ball is hit. If you wait until the ball hits the front wall or crosses the service line, it may be too late to get into position.

As the server contacts the ball, your first movement is to pivot and step toward the side of the court where you think the serve will land. The pivot, or turn of your body, must be completed simultaneously with the initial stepping action or you will lose too much time.

Cross Over or Step Out

You have two choices of first-step mechanics during your pivot. For a backhand return (assuming you're right handed) you may pivot, cross over and step with your right foot, and then contact the ball; or you may pivot, step out first with the left foot, and then cross over with the right foot. Either technique (illustrated in Figure 9.2) is good and both are quick. The crossover step is one long stride. If you use the initial step-out, keep it a short step and follow with a long crossover stride. The crossover is quicker if the ball can be played with one step, but if you need extended reach you should step out and cross over.

Some players use short shuffle steps to move into the return-of-serve hitting position. This is fine if the distance you have to move to the ball is short. But the shuffle step for most players is more time consuming than the step-out and crossover patterns.

Moving to return serves on the forehand side, for the right-handed player, uses the same principle as the backhand return except that you cross over with the left foot and step out with the right foot. In

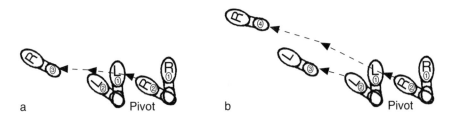

a   Pivot   b   Pivot

Figure 9.2   The three phases of the crossover footwork for the return of serve (a) and the four phases of the step-out footwork for the return of serve (b). Both illustrations depict a right-handed receiver returning a ball hit to the backhand side.

all cases the speed, angle, and direction of the serve should determine the angle of your movement pattern. The faster the serve, the quicker you must move to successfully return the serve. You do need to think of your comfort zone when selecting your movement patterns for service returns.

Move, Be Set, Then Hit

As you move you should stay slightly crouched and attempt to get your racquet back into the backswing quickly. The slightly crouched position keeps you closer to low serves and allows you to extend your body and legs into the return shot. You should also be concentrating on the ball while you are moving into position for the return of service. The ideal sequence is to move, get set (as Woody demonstrates in Figure 9.3), and then hit the ball. However, you often do not have enough time to do this, and you must play the service return without being able to set up. In this case the best return is to the ceiling.

SERVICE RETURN SHOTS

The major return-of-service shots are the ceiling shot, the pass, and the kill. These can be hit on the bounce or can be volley returns.

Ceiling Returns

The ceiling shot is the best percentage return on any service ball coming to you that does not afford an offensive opportunity. It can

Figure 9.3 Here Woody has moved into position in time to set up for a powerful return.

also be used effectively on hard drive serves. The ceiling return gives you a greater margin for error and should also force your opponent out of center-court position. Most players prefer to have the ceiling return end up in the back backhand corner (as shown in Figure 9.4). The chances are good that the return of your service return will also be a ceiling shot. As mentioned in chapter 7, although many players feel the ceiling shot is strictly defensive, we feel that it can be used offensively, and in returning service it can be used either way. It is defensive if you are digging for the serves, but if you're set to hit the shot well (as shown in Figure 9.5) it can be offensive, forcing the server to the defense.

Passing Returns

As shown in Figure 9.6 (page 157), the passing shot can be employed either down-the-wall or crosscourt, and either passing shot should

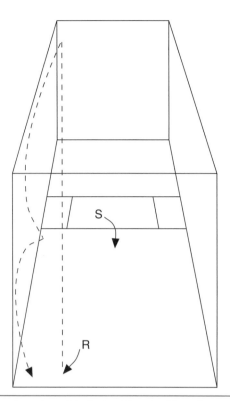

Figure 9.4 Return of service with the backhand ceiling shot.

be tried if the serve gives you an easy return. Any time the server gives you a serve that you can hit offensively, you must make use of the advantage.

Kill Returns and Variations

The kill return is very effective off a poorly placed drive serve that is coming at you low and hard. If the drive serve comes out to center court, go for the kill.

You can use other variations for service returns including ceiling shots to the backhand corner, Z-ball returns, volley service returns, and just about any other return shot that either wins a point or forces the server out of center-court position.

Figure 9.5   Woody sets up and delivers an offensive overhand ceiling shot return.

Volley Returns

The volley service return is effective because it gives the server less time to set up in center-court position. You can hit ceilings, kills, or passes off the volley service return, and by using this return you often catch the server off balance. The volley return is also one of the most effective returns against a lob serve. You should volley the lob serve before it forces you into a high backhand shot from the corner. When volleying a lob serve, you must adhere to the safety zone rule by staying behind the receiving line. The rule indicates that you can follow through with your swing, but no part of your body can follow through over the receiving line. This rule has been adopted for safety purposes and to keep the lob serve as a viable part of an ever-increasing power game.

Some players use what is called a *quick service return*, which is similar to other service returns except that you always return the serve as soon as possible to give the server less time to get center-court position. The volley service return is an effective quick service return. When using the quick service return, do not allow the serve

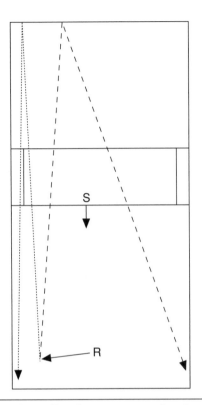

Figure 9.6 Both down-the-wall and crosscourt passing shots can be effective, offensive service returns.

to go by you. The quick service return not only surprises the server, but it also gives the receiver less time to react to the ball. You may also short hop a lob serve by hitting the ball early. If you use this technique, shoot for passing shots not kills. For most players there is too little margin for error in going for kills at this time. With the volley or short hop service return, you are aggressively forcing your opponent out of center court with an offensive shot. This is an advanced-level shot.

SERVICE RETURN STRATEGY

As you await the serve, you should be thinking offensive return. You're looking to prevent the server from getting to center court. But, if the server gives you a setup, go ahead and take it with a kill or a pass and win the rally outright. If your opponent's serve is good, then pick the ceiling return, which gives you time to get into position and forces your opponent out of center court.

Keep constant pressure on the server so that he or she feels you will put away any poorly hit serve. Don't be foolish and try to score on every return, but don't sit back and allow setups to go by. Also, hit a variety of service returns to keep the server off balance.

Decide which type of return is best to use against the server before the serve is put into play, but also remember that the type and the precision of the serve will affect your return options. You will need to be able to change your strategy quickly depending on the serve itself.

Key Elements for Service Returns

- Return offensive serves with ceiling and passing shots; return less effective serves with kill shots.

- Position yourself to receive the serve according to the ability and the strategies of both you and the server.

- Be light on your feet when receiving the serve; remember that it is easier to move if you are already in motion.

Taking Your Game to Its Highest Level   *Woody Clouse*

The first priority on return of serve is to remove your opponent from center court.

- Always give yourself a chance to win each rally.

- Don't go for flat roll-outs on your service return.

- Always go to the ceiling when you're forced off balance.

Drill for Return of Serves

Offensive and Defensive Return Drill (With Partner)

Purpose:

To practice both offensive and defensive returns of service.

Directions:

Position yourself to receive and have your partner hit ten consecutive drive serves to your backhand corner; attempt to return as many as possible offensively and play the rest defensively.

Variations:

A. Have your partner hit only lob serves or Z serves and repeat the drill.

B. Have your partner hit all defensive serves and return all serves offensively.

C. Have your partner hit all offensive serves and return all serves defensively.

D. Repeat the drills for your forehand service return.

Chapter 10

Advanced Shots and Skills

Photo by Jim Warner—KILLSHOT magazine

*A*s you progress toward the intermediate and advanced levels of skill, you will add a variety of new weapons to your repertoire of shots. You cannot continue to increase your skill level without mastering these shots. This chapter introduces and analyzes the more advanced skills you will need to round out your game.

OVERHEAD SHOTS

Thus far we have stressed the importance of patience on most offensive shots; you should usually wait for the ball to get low before playing it. The overhead, however, is an offensive shot that is played high rather than low and it can be a valuable option. Overhead passing and kill shots have a low success rate because anytime you attempt to play a ball high and bring it down low on the front wall you have a high chance of error. However, game situations occur when having the overhead shot at your disposal is a definite plus. Overhead passing shots give you a greater margin for error than overhead kills. On all overhead shots you need to be set early for the shot and your opponent should be out of position on the court.

The racquetball overhead is usually a forehand shot similar in mechanics to the tennis serve, and it is often effective against a short ceiling shot. Backhand overheads can also be effective but are difficult to execute because most players are weaker on backhand shots. Because the overhead is normally played on a high-bouncing ball, you usually have time to maneuver into a forehand hitting position. It is used effectively to break up a ceiling-ceiling rally. The element of surprise is important to the success of offensive overheads. Many of your overhead shots will be ceiling shots (see chapter 7). Use the overhead passing or kill shot when your opponent is deep in the court anticipating more ceiling returns. Make these shots resemble the overhead ceiling shot—disguise as well as surprise!

As Figure 10.1 demonstrates, the difference between the ceiling overhead and the overhead pass or kill is the position of the racquet on ball contact. For the ceiling shot you contact the ball even with or slightly behind the body. But in the overhead pass or kill, you contact the ball slightly in front of the body, which causes your racquet face to close and imparts the needed downward angle on the high-bouncing ball.

Overhead Position

Position yourself sideways so that the upper body can rotate at the waist providing the power needed for these shots. As you begin the shot, your weight should be on the back foot. Your arm should be moving in the typical overhand throwing motion used in the overhand ceiling shot. Begin shifting your weight to the front foot as your

Figure 10.1 The similarities and differences between the ceiling shot (a) and the overhead pass or kill (b).

hitting arm comes forward. As you contact the ball, the weight should be shifted to the front foot, the upper body should rotate, the wrist should rotate and flex, and the legs should extend. Use a full backswing and a natural follow-through. Play the ball in front of your body so that you can take the high ball low to the front wall.

Overhead Passing Shot

The overhead passing shot can be hit crosscourt or down the wall, but be sure that the down-the-wall shot hugs, but does not hit, the side wall. If the ball hits the side wall it will rebound into the middle backcourt and give your opponent—who is already in the backcourt awaiting ceiling shots—a setup. Power is important in the overhead pass because of the great distance the ball must travel. You should use the overhead passing shot to win the point outright or to set up a weak return by your opponent so that you can put the next shot away.

Overhead Kills

The overhead kill is effective with a little less power than the overhead passing shot because the ball travels less distance and because you would like a short rebound. Use the front corners for success in the overhead kill. Hitting the corners slows the shot significantly and causes unexpected rebound angles. This change of speed and direction results from the steep angle of the shot and is critical to its success. If you miss the corner, the ball may rebound very high to the midcourt area and give your opponent a setup.

Key Elements for the Overhead Shot

- Use overhead shots sparingly.
- It is difficult to successfully hit a high ball low to the front wall.
- Use the overhead as a surprise tactic during ceiling rallies and against other short, high shots.
- Overhead shots are most effective when your opponent is out of position on the court.
- Speed and accuracy are critical for the success of offensive overhead shots.

Taking Your Game to Its Highest Level   *Woody Clouse*

The overhead can be a very effective offensive weapon but is the lowest percentage shot in the game.

- If you're not set, go to the ceiling.
- If you are set, you have four options for hitting the overhead: a) the down-the-wall; b) crosscourt; c) pinch; and d) reverse pinch.

PINCH SHOT

The pinch shot is a variation of the kill shot; it hits the side wall before it hits the front wall. The pinch can be hit as a backhand, forehand, splat, volley, or as a reverse pinch. It is most effective when you are in the frontcourt close to one of the side walls and you play the ball to the closest side wall as seen in Figure 10.2. Two factors make the pinch a useful offensive weapon. When the ball hits the side wall, the speed of the ball decreases and it rebounds slowly out of the corner. Also, because the ball hits the side wall first, it rebounds off the front wall across the court rather than toward the backcourt. The pinch shot is one of the few shots that, when hit correctly, takes its second bounce before it reaches the front service line. This quick second bounce makes the pinch an awesome weapon.

The pinch shot is a good way to change the game's pace. A soft-touch pinch is similar to a drop shot and is effective when your opponent is hugging the back wall.

The backhand pinch is somewhat more difficult than the forehand pinch. Remember to use all of your power sources when hitting backhand pinches. Some individuals have a tendency to push the pinch rather than hit it. To avoid pushing the ball, imagine the side wall as the front wall and hit the ball into the side with power. You

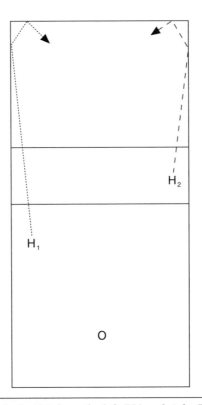

Figure 10.2 The pinch shot hit from the left (H_1) and right (H_2) sides of the court.

would not push a front-wall kill shot; this technique may help you hit through the ball properly.

You can occasionally hit pinches from the backcourt, but you must be accurate; otherwise, you may give your opponent a setup in center court. The backcourt pinch should be used sparingly and mainly to catch your opponent off guard.

Hitting Position

Your basic hitting position for the pinch is similar to your position for hitting kill and passing shots (see chapter 6). However, you should contact the ball slightly forward of the body plane on forehand pinches, and slightly behind the body plane on the backhand pinch. The ball should hit the side wall anywhere from two inches to six feet from the front wall depending on your position in relation to the side wall. Remember, it is more effective to hit the pinch to the close side of the court.

The pinch is most effective when your opponent is behind you because you can legally screen the ball for an instant, which often helps you win the rally. Hitting the shot with ample power is important. Also, keeping the ball low is critical to prevent a rebound into center court and a setup. It is also good to pinch to your opponent's side of the court since the ball will travel away, rather than towards, your opponent.

Splats

The splat is a hard, elongated pinch shot. The ball is contacted close to a side wall and is hit into the side wall near where you originally contacted the ball. The ball usually has a large amount of spin on it that causes it to be unpredictable when it comes off the front wall.

The ball is hit like a parallel passing shot, but it glances off the side wall and becomes a type of pinch. The glancing off the side wall imparts excessive spin to the ball that can cause the ball to react like a perfect pinch, streak down through the center of the court, or spin off the front wall in a crosscourt pass. You can play a wide-angle splat by hitting the side wall farther from the front corner (see Figure 10.3). In any case, the splat receives its name from the distinctive "splat" sound it makes when it hits into the front wall. The splat is a power shot and if not accurately placed can come off the front wall and set up your opponent.

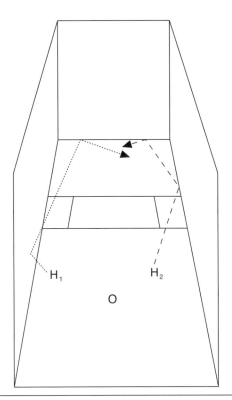

Figure 10.3 The wide-angle splat from the left (H_1) and from the right (H_2).

Reverse Pinches

Most pinch shots are hit into the side wall that is nearer you. You may also go crosscourt with your pinch for the reverse pinch as seen in Figure 10.4. When using this shot, play the ball slightly behind the body plane on the forehand side and slightly in front of the body plane on the backhand side. Beginners and intermediate-level players use the reverse pinch more than advanced players because crosscourt shots in general are preferred by beginning players.

Pinch Volleys

Like volley shots in general, the pinch volley is difficult to execute because of decreased reaction time. However, the pinch volley changes the pace of the game, and it will often catch your opponent off guard and allow you to win a point outright. It is, therefore, well worth the effort to master the shot. You need a compact swing on the

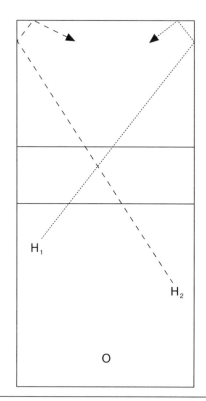

Figure 10.4   The reverse pinch from the left (H$_1$) and from the right (H$_2$).

pinch volley, with a short backswing and short follow-through. A firm grip, upper-body rotation, low center of gravity, and an intense focus on the ball are all vital for hitting successful pinch volleys. As usual, the pinch volley is most useful when your opponent is either behind or alongside you as seen in Figure 10.5.

Key Elements for the Pinch Shot

- Use the pinch when you are in front of your opponent or when your opponent cannot easily move forward.
- Hit the pinch with accuracy and keep the shot low.
- Don't push the backhand pinch; swing through the shot normally.
- Use the pinch as a change of pace.

Taking Your Game to Its Highest Level *Woody Clouse*

- Pinches are a much lower percentage shot than passing shots.
- Use passes much more than pinches.
- If your opponent is leaning back or is not paying attention, hit the pinch that you feel will end the rally.

RETURNING WALLPAPER SHOTS

The wallpaper shot is any ball coming off the front or back wall that acts like it is glued to a side wall as seen in Figure 10.6. The ball is so close to the side wall that it is difficult to get a racquet on it. All of us

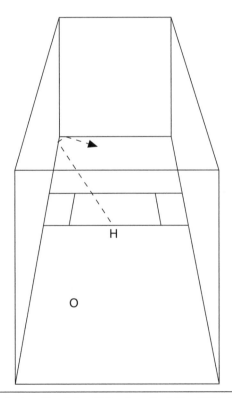

Figure 10.5 The pinch volley is best hit when the hitter (H) is in center court and the opponent (O) is behind the hitter.

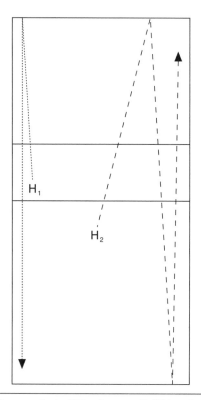

Figure 10.6   The wallpaper shot off the front wall (H_1) and off the back wall (H_2).

have had to return a wallpaper shot at some time. Because of its closeness to the side wall and because it often will hit the wall and kick out unexpectedly, it's a tough shot. What do you do?

The Defensive Wallpaper Return

The chances of hitting a good return off a wallpaper shot are probably about one in five for the intermediate-level player and about three or four in five for the advanced-level player. You cannot attack a wallpaper shot by trying to blast it with all your power. Even if you get your racquet on the ball and hit it hard, you will probably set up your opponent. Think defensively, slow down your swing, and attempt to control the ball. These tactics allow you the best chance of a successful return.

You must also allow yourself enough room between the side wall and your body so that you can swing fluidly. Many players stand too close to the side wall when returning a wallpaper shot, and hitting from an awkward, cramped position makes the return more difficult (see Figure 10.7). Also, if you are too close to the wall and the ball jumps off it, you have less time to react than if you position yourself farther from the wall. You should be an arm's length from the wall.

Because the wall sometimes prevents you from taking a full swing, the ceiling and wallpaper returns are your best percentage shots in returning a wallpaper shot. Hitting a wallpaper shot return is something like trying to catch a fly along a wall with your hand; you would slide your hand along the wall and scoop up the fly. Use the same technique in racquetball. Use a shorter backswing and shorter follow-through because of the wall. The racquet head may be perpendicular or parallel to the side wall depending on your positioning (see Figure 10.8). The parallel position usually puts more of the racquet face closer to the wall and gives you a better chance of returning the shot, but this technique is more difficult to time and to measure your distance from the wall. As with most shots your comfort zone will dictate your positioning. The shape of your racquet head will also help determine your swing and racquet face position.

Figure 10.7   Don't get cramped in your swing for the wallpaper shot.

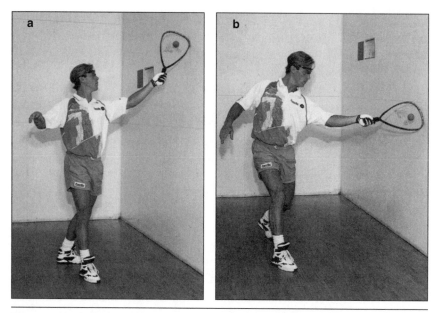

Figure 10.8   Whether you return a wallpaper shot with the racquet head nearly parallel (a) or perpendicular (b) to the wall, keep a full arm's length away from the wall.

You should place the largest, flattest surface of your racquet head along the wall.

The Offensive Wallpaper Return

If you can return a wallpaper shot with a wallpaper shot, you place all the difficulties we have been describing on your opponent's shoulders. This shot is extremely difficult to execute because if the ball hits the side wall it will probably result in a setup for your opponent. Because the same consideration applies to down-the-wall and ceiling shots, you may find that practicing these shots will help you play an offensive wallpaper return more effectively.

AROUND-THE-WALL SHOT

The around-the-wall shot is a crosscourt shot that travels around the court and ends up deep on the side of the court from where it was

---

Key Elements for the Wallpaper Shot

- Think of scooping or catching a fly off the side wall as you return the wallpaper shot.
- Slow down, think defense, don't cramp yourself, and get the largest portion of your racquet face next to the wall when returning a wallpaper shot.
- Focus on the ball and attempt to play it an arm's length away.

---

originally hit. The around-the-wall shot can be compared to the Z serve; the difference is that the around-the-wall shot hits the side wall before it hits the front wall. Use this shot offensively to change tempo and unbalance your opponent or to break up a ceiling rally. Defensively, the around-the-wall ball gives you time to regain good position because it travels such a long, high distance.

The Around-the-Wall Flight Plan

The around-the-wall shot is played when you are in or near one of the back corners. Hit the shot between 10 and 16 feet high on the near side wall and 3 or 4 feet from the front wall. The angle carries the ball against the front wall, then to the far side wall around service-area deep; the ball then angles crosscourt and first bounces about two thirds of the way crosscourt and ends up near the back corner (see Figure 10.9). The ball is in midair most of the way across the court and is slanting downward. Hit the shot with medium force. If you initiate the shot from the forehand side, it will end up on the forehand side and vice versa for the backhand.

Hitting Around-the-Wall Shots

You can hit the around-the-wall shot underhand, sidearm, or overhead. The key to success is to hit the ball at moderate speed with the appropriate angle to the side wall target area. Hit the overhand with stroke mechanics similar to the overhead offensive shot and the overhand ceiling shot.

The three major errors in hitting the around-the-wall shot are hitting the ceiling, hitting too hard, or hitting the incorrect angle to

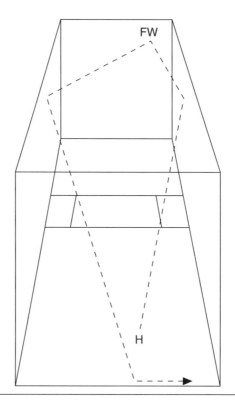

Figure 10.9   The around-the-wall ball.

the first side wall. Hitting the ceiling causes the ball to come straight down in the frontcourt and gives your opponent a setup. If you hit the ball too hard, it will eventually hit the back wall and come out for a setup for your opponent. Hitting the ball off the first side wall at an incorrect angle will cause the ball to drop short or fly long.

You will hit around-the-wall shots with both forehands and backhands. Because of the low margin for error, use the shot sparingly. You can successfully play the shot as a change of pace, as a substitute for a ceiling shot, or as a defensive shot to give you time to gain good court position.

Defending Around-the-Wall Shots

The best defense against the around-the-wall shot is to step into the center backcourt area and to play the ball on a volley. A passing shot is the best strategy in this situation. Beginners sometimes stand flat-

> ## Key Elements for the Around-the-Wall Shot
>
> - Use the around-the-wall shot as a change of pace or to break up a ceiling rally.
>
> ### Taking Your Game to Its Highest Level *Woody Clouse*
>
> - Hit this shot off a "get" in which a ceiling shot is not possible.
> - Today's touring pros are too good at stepping up and cutting off the ball for you to hit a winner on the around-the-wall shot.
> - Use it to regain good court position.
> - Use medium speed and careful placement, but play the shot sparingly.
> - Ceiling shots are better than the around-the-wall shot because they have a greater margin for error.

footedly and watch the ball as it caroms around the walls until it is too late to react. Don't let the ball hypnotize you; decide where the ball is best played, move into that court position, and play it.

DROP SHOTS

The drop shot is an effective weapon anywhere on the court; however, the best situation in which to use it is when you are in the frontcourt and your opponent is in the backcourt as seen in Figure 10.10. It is an offensive shot designed to end the rally or to win the point. If you don't end the point with the drop shot, your opponent probably will on the return. The drop is a touch shot; the slightest mistake in its execution will cause the ball to either skip on the floor or hit too hard or high on the front wall and give your opponent a setup, so use this shot sparingly.

We suggest using kills or pinches when you are in the frontcourt, and occasionally adding a drop shot. The drop shot is an effective offensive shot when used at the proper time in the correct manner against the right opponent.

The hitting mechanics for the drop shot are similar to those for passing and kill shots. If you change your stroking patterns for a drop

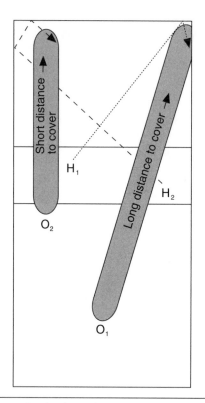

Figure 10.10   The drop shot hit from the service area with the opponent up (O_2) and (the better of the two choices) with the opponent back (O_1).

shot, your opponent may notice the change and be able to anticipate your drop shot.

How do you make the drop shot look like a hard-driven pass or kill? Let's consider three basic techniques for disguising drop shots.

1. **Decrease your backswing.** Very slightly decrease your backswing. As you contact the ball use no wrist action; bring your forward arm movement almost to a halt at ball impact, and follow through less than normal. The key to success with this technique is to make the drop shot look like other strokes and hit with the correct touch—neither too hard nor too soft. Practice is the way to perfect this technique of dropping.

2. **Cut through the ball from a slightly high to low swing.** Don't overdo the swing or you'll tip your opponent. The swing itself has velocity like a pass or kill shot, but as contact is made the force of the racquet is directed more towards the floor than the front wall. This

high-to-low hitting action imparts backspin to the ball and greatly reduces its forward speed, thus giving you a soft touch on your drop. The more you cut through the ball going from high to low, the more force is imparted down and the less force is imparted forward.

3. **Relax your grip as you contact the ball.** The relaxed grip allows the ball to rebound off the racquet face with little power, which results in a soft shot. This is the most difficult technique to master; therefore, it is the least desirable of the three.

You may also combine aspects of the three drop-shot techniques and be successful in softly contacting the ball. Remember, the key to the drop shot is deception and touch, and the best time to use it is when you are in the frontcourt and the opponent is in the backcourt. The drop shot should not be a push. If you push the ball your opponent will know that a drop shot is coming.

When to Drop

You may play a drop shot off a pass, a volley, a back-wall shot, a kill, or any other poorly hit shot. Hitting off a kill is tricky because the ball is coming extremely fast, and it is sometimes difficult to slow the shot down into a soft drop shot. The best time to hit a drop shot is when you do not have to move very far to reach the ball. If you are in motion, the speed of body movement makes the drop shot even more difficult to execute.

Drop shots are effective against an opponent who has trouble moving forward or who has slow reaction time or who lacks concentration. They are also excellent against the opponent who stays in the backcourt or who has a tendency to sit back on his or her heels during rallies. Drop shots can frustrate an opponent who is slow or tiring. If the opponent is in center court, but does not turn to watch your return, you can successfully use a drop shot. This is, however, the only situation in which you want to try the drop shot when your opponent is in front of you.

Drop Shot Placement

The best placement of the drop shot is into the corners with a trajectory similar to a kill or pinch. The use of the corners helps slow the ball and thus gives a more effective drop shot. Hit drop shots

---

Key Elements for the Drop Shot

- Use drop shots sporadically when your opponent is in the backcourt.
- You must be deceptive with your drop shot or your opponent will have a setup.
- Hit drop shots into the corners because they slow the shot down and accentuate the touch aspect of the shot.

---

from knee level or below and keep the ball low on the front wall. You can hit drop shots from a high, even overhead, position, but this makes the drop shot more difficult to execute because the ball going from high to low has a tendency to bounce high after it hits the floor, giving your opponent time to get to the ball. Remember, the drop shot must die in the front corners; if it doesn't, your opponent will probably put the ball away.

The Back-Wall Drop Shot

Another variation of the drop shot can be used against beginning or intermediate players who hit the ball hard and high. Use it when you are within a few feet of the front wall playing a hard rebound off the back wall and your opponent is in center court or backcourt. As you hit the ball, you actually slow its forward momentum and make it drop into the corners. The technique is to get your racquet in front of the ball, between the front wall and the ball, and to slow the ball by letting it slide across your racquet face. This must be done with precise timing and touch so it is not a carry or sling. You are moving in the same direction as the ball, so the actual slinging is unnoticeable. It is a legal hit in most official's eyes.

QUICK-DRAW FOREHANDS AND BACKHANDS

Sometimes a ball comes at you after hitting a crotch or takes a freak bounce, and you cannot set up to hit it with correct mechanics. Nevertheless, you need to adjust and hit an offensive shot. This shot is termed a quick-draw forehand or backhand.

Because you do not have time to set up, the wrist becomes the major source of power. Keep the wrist flexible, almost rubbery; you cannot apply any power to this shot with a stiff wrist. The swing is much shorter than the regular forehand swing. Use a bullwhip or towel-snapping backhand action with little follow-through. You will not have time to get your body and feet turned sideways, so you will have to exaggerate upper-body rotation and shifting of your weight from your heels to your toes to obtain some extra force.

When using this shot, racquet-ball contact often occurs behind your ideal hitting position. This creates problems of accuracy and control. Hitting too late may be caused by two factors. First, you may have reacted late because of the unpredictability of the shot itself. Second, you may have let the ball get past the correct hitting position to give yourself a little extra time. You can solve these problems by practicing shots using less footwork movement than usual and hitting the ball with a quicker than normal action. Work on and stress the rubbery-flexible wrist action. As you practice quick-draw shots, put yourself in an awkward position when hitting, but try to make the stroke fluid by using extra wrist action.

Your forward stride can also help or hinder your forehand or backhand shot. Many beginners step forward with the lead foot while keeping the toes pointed at the side wall, which limits upper-body rotation. If you angle your foot forward when you step forward, as seen in Figure 10.11, the upper body can rotate farther, thus providing more power in the swing. The increase in upper body rotation is caused by opening the hips, which allows for greater range of motion. The action on the forehand side can be compared to throwing a flat stone so that it skips across water. The backhand action can be compared to throwing a Frisbee.

HALF-VOLLEY

The half-volley is an option for playing a ball that hits close to your feet. It is not really a volley, but the ball is played almost immediately after it bounces. You play it on the short hop. The half-volley is defensive when it is the only way you can play a ball at your feet and you are attempting only to return it to the front wall. It can also be used offensively like a volley to catch your opponent off guard and to give him or her less time to react to the ball.

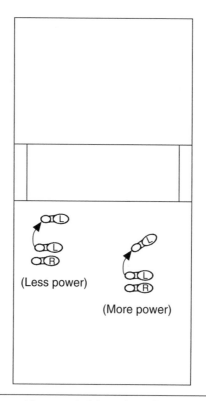

Figure 10.11   Stepping with an angled front foot allows for more upper body rotation and therefore gives the hitter more power.

You can hit passing shots, kill shots, and ceiling shots off a half-volley. The best body position is facing a side wall, but you can also play this shot facing the front wall. Getting yourself low is important for passing and kill half-volleys, but not so important for the ceiling half-volley. Use any appropriate grip and bend at your knees. Keep your back straight and keep your racquet head up unless you are going to the ceiling. Lean your weight into the stroke; you will probably not be able to step into the ball because it is already close to your feet. Keep your head down to watch the ball; if you lift your head, your body will rise, your swing will rise, and the ball will hit high on the front wall. Use a shorter than normal backswing and follow-through because you have so little time to react. You can practice half-volleying by taking balls on the short hop during practice.

Z SHOT

The Z shot is similar to the Z serve. Hit Z shots sparingly because unless you can hit a perfect Z with the ball ending up hugging and running parallel to the back wall, it can set up your opponent. Z shots may be used defensively to give you time to get back in position, or they can be used offensively as a change of pace.

The Z shot should be hit from the backcourt area to the front wall 15 to 16 feet high in the corner; the ball hits the side wall quickly and carries diagonally crosscourt, hits the opposite side wall three feet to a few inches from the back wall, and then rebounds parallel to the back wall, as seen in Figure 10.12. This makes return shots difficult. The Z shot is effective against beginners because they become confused when the ball rebounds off several walls. Against more advanced opponents, the Z shot is less effective because they can read the ball's angle and ending points. Unless the Z shot is creeping along the back wall, an advanced player will put it away.

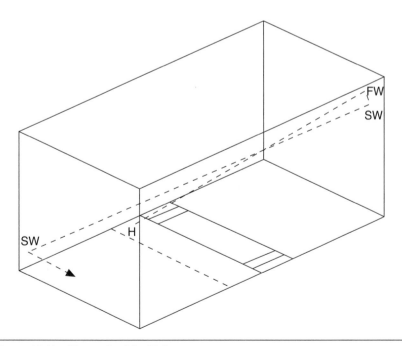

Figure 10.12 The path of the Z shot.

COMBINATION SHOTS

Shots that combine two or more basic techniques are called combination shots. Every racquetball player hits an unorthodox shot that can be played for a winner. You can combine shots, for example, by trying overheads on what are usually underhand shots, by hitting shots in the frontcourt that are normally hit from the backcourt, or by driving shots with power that are customarily returned with control. You should also consider hitting shots at strange angles and with odd spins, and don't forget the oddball shot that may use too many or too few walls to accomplish its purpose.

When employed in the right situation, combination shots will place your opponent on the defense, give you time to regain good court position, or win a point or service for you. Some shots described previously are actually combination shots: the splat, the reverse ceiling, the Z shot, and the back-wall—back-wall shot. Try to hit an overhead pinch or reverse pinch in the backcourt or in center court, with power or with touch, or try hitting a backcourt drop reverse pinch. These shots have all been hit at one time or another but have never been discussed or written about at length. Combination shots are fun, practical, and creative. In a strange rally situation or an unfamiliar court position, step forward and try your combination shot to continue the rally or to win a point.

TRICK SHOTS

Most trick shots are awkward, last-ditch shots, but you can hit winners with them—demoralizing winners. They can be played by combining movements and skills when you are caught in an unfavorable position, and by practicing trick shots you can increase your percentage of winners.

One of the more common trick shots is the between-the-legs shot, which can be hit as a kill, pass, pinch, or even as a ceiling shot. Trick shots can be defensive or offensive. If you can hit a good between-the-legs kill, you not only score a point but also may demoralize your opponent. The between-the-legs shot is usually employed when you have mispositioned yourself or when the ball takes a freaky bounce off the back wall or side wall. Let's say that a back-wall shot is coming right at you and that you are inadvertently facing the back wall. You allow the ball to drop down between your legs, and then you hit a forehand flick-shot through the legs to the side of the front wall as seen in Figure 10.13. A flicking action is used because you have no time or space for a windup and follow-through. You can modify this shot by lifting one leg so that a larger opening is available through which to hit the ball.

Another trick shot is a forehand backhand. This shot is executed when you are attempting to play a ball on your backhand side that has gone deep into the court, and you are moving toward the back wall. The ball takes a strange bounce, and all you can do is hit the ball as you are facing the back wall with the forehand face of your racquet on the backhand side of the body. It is usually an underhand shot as seen in Figure 10.14.

Another trick shot is the behind-the-back shot. It is usually executed from the normal backhand side when you are facing the back wall or side wall, and you contact the ball with the forehand face or backhand face of the racquet as seen in Figure 10.15. This is also a flick-shot because of difficult body positioning.

Figure 10.13 Between the legs.

Figure 10.14   The forehand backhand.

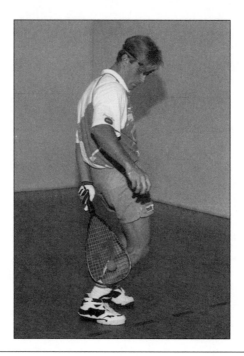

Figure 10.15   Behind the back.

KEEPING TO THE CORNERS

Let's now consider the importance of placing your shots in the back corners. What we mean by the back corner is a three-foot cube shown in Figure 10.16. You should hit your ceiling shots, passing shots, lobs, and serves into the back corners. The first offensive advantage is that it makes your opponent hit a long distance to the front wall, producing a greater chance for error. Second, if your shot stays in the corner cube, the opponent must contend with both the back and side walls in taking his or her swing. Third, a ball hitting in the corner can take odd bounces and angles, which can further frustrate the opponent. Fourth, hitting to the corners also enables you to take and hold center-court position. Even if your shot to the corner is less than perfect, it may be difficult to return if it comes out running parallel to and hugging the back wall.

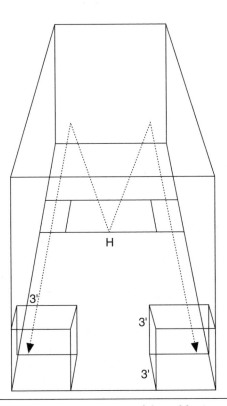

Figure 10.16 The corner cube areas are two of the gold mines of the court.

What are the best techniques for returning a ball out of the corners? Most of the time a good corner shot will force you to be defensive; a good option is the ceiling shot. When the ball goes into the corner, be patient, decide where it is going to end, and position yourself for the best possible return. Deciding where to position yourself will depend on your ability to remember rebound angles. If you do not know the angles, you must practice hitting balls into the corner. Attempt to understand and remember the angles as you return practice shots out of the corner.

Occasionally it is to your advantage to play a ball while it is moving through the back corner rather than waiting until it begins to come out. If you think that the ball is going to rebound hugging a wall, it might be easier to play it in the corner.

Your footwork is important in playing corner shots. If you are overanxious, you will be jammed into the corner. Be patient and play corner balls with backhands on the backhand side of the body. Don't try to play them with forehands by running around your backhand. Take controlled steps and employ shuffle steps, crossover, and step-out approaches to reach the ball. Remember that if you have to contend with the back wall and side wall, you may have to slightly alter your ideal hitting position to bring the ball out of the corner with a good return. With all wall shots your ideal hitting position is arm's length from the closest wall.

SHOT ANALYSIS CHARTS

A shot analysis chart is a means of recording the types of shots you hit, where you hit them, and their success in a match. It will give you a good indication of where you performed well and where you had difficulty, and you can use this information to improve your point output. You must have a coach or friend record your shots for you, and because the ball travels so fast it is possible that not all shots will be marked. Two recorders can do a more thorough job, with each recorder having responsibilities only for certain shots. If two recorders are impracticable, one person recording as many shots as possible will still give you a useful analysis of your game. The recordings must be accurate; it may be best to record only one skill during each playing session.

Reviewing the analysis chart can be very helpful in improving your game. For example, if you find that you were successful on 25 percent of your backhand kill attempts and 85 percent of your forehand passing shots, you will know that you have to work hard on backhand kills in practice but spend much less time on forehand passing shots.

Tables 10.1 and 10.2 show sample shot analysis charts for serves, return of serves, and passing shots. You can design your own chart for other skills such as overheads, pinches, lobs, and drop shots. In any case, use the chart to record the total number of shots you hit, your percentage of forehands, and your percentage of winners.

DIVING

Some players believe that diving is an integral part of the advanced player's shot repertoire, but other players say that diving is not needed at any level of play. Diving takes much effort and energy and after diving you are usually out of position.

The major controversy over diving centers upon injuries. Those who recommend diving say that injury is a part of the game; those who reject diving declare that it is foolish to intentionally risk injury. You will have to make your decision whether diving should be a part of your game or not.

The basic purpose behind diving is to reach a ball that would be otherwise unretrievable. In most cases a dive is solely a defensive shot; however, you occasionally can hit offensively from a dive.

If you choose to dive, reserve the maneuver for crucial points such as tiebreakers or the end of close games. If the score is 10-10, an all-out effort in the form of a dive might decide the outcome of the game. In addition, if your opponent is not used to diving, the shot can be a change of pace that may help win the game. Scores of 0-0, 5-2, or even 10-2 would not warrant diving. The importance of the game should also help you decide whether to dive or not. If it is in the first round of an insignificant tournament, diving is probably not called for; but near the finals of an important tournament, the diving tactic might be worthwhile.

Apart from the risk of injury, diving takes a great deal of energy, and on many dive returns you are on the floor out of position while

Table 10.1 Serve and Return of Serve Analysis

Player _____

Match _____ Date _____ Court # and Type _____

Game #1 _____ #2 _____ #3 _____ Win _____ Loss _____

	1st Serves				2nd Serves				Return of Serves		
	Drive	Lob	Z	Combo	Drive	Lob	Z	Combo	Passing	Kill	Ceiling
Number of shots											
Number of successful shots											
Number of winners											
Number of aces											
Number of points lost											

Table 10.2 Passing Shot Analysis

Player _____

Match _____ Date _____ Court # and Type _____

Game #1 _____ #2 _____ #3 _____ Win _____ Loss _____

	Down-the-Wall		Crosscourt		Wide-Angle	
	Forehand	Backhand	Forehand	Backhand	Forehand	Backhand
Number of shots						
Number of successful shots						
Number of winners						
Number of aces						
Number of points lost						

your opponent easily puts away your return. Also, when you dive and are on the floor in front of or close to your opponent, being called for an avoidable hinder is a good possibility.

Dive Preparation

Let's look at the safest techniques to prevent injury while diving and still retrieve the ball. Diving can be divided into preparation, the dive itself, and the recovery phase. Begin the preparation phase in a semicrouched position as shown by Woody in Figure 10-17a. Take a step or steps as needed depending on how far you have to move to reach the ball; then lean into the dive and powerfully extend your legs to push off the floor. You should be fully extended and relatively parallel and low to the ground.

The Dive

While you are in the air, you should have your racquet out in front of you in a jabbing motion for safety as well as for maximum reach. Having your racquet well in front of you also saves time. You will not usually have time to take a backswing, so you need to have your racquet set quickly. Almost immediately after contacting the ball, you will be approaching your landing. Have your nonhitting hand near your body. As you are landing, place this hand on the floor to absorb, along with your chest, the impact of the fall (see Figure 10.17b).

You should hit the floor with your back arched to keep your head and knees away from the impact area. You want to land on the chest area of the body, and because you will be traveling forward through the air as you land, you can slide slightly in the direction of the dive. This sliding action also helps to absorb some of the shock impact as shown by Woody in Figure 10.17c. Women players must avoid landing on the chest because of the danger of breast injury. Do not hit the floor with any unpadded body parts. Elbows, knees, hips, shoulders, and the head should not hit the court floor. Also, never dive near the side or front walls because the impact of your head, shoulder, or leg with the wall could cause serious injury. Hitting a wall while diving is totally different from hitting the floor and should never be done.

With the shot completed, you have to recover because your opponent (though impressed with your gutsiness) will probably be

Figure 10.17 Begin the preparation phase of the dive from a semicrouched position (a). Make contact by jabbing at the ball. Use your landing hand as a shock absorber (b). When your body makes contact with the floor, let yourself slide a little with the dive (c). Then get your hands and feet together and pick yourself up to play the next shot (d).

Key Elements for the Dive

- Keep diving to a minimum to help avoid injury.
- Dive low and absorb the landing with a slide, the chest, and the nonhitting hand. Land on a padded body part.
- Don't dive into or near side walls or front walls.
- Recover quickly after you dive.
- Hit mostly ceiling shots off the dive.

Taking Your Game to Its Highest Level _____ *Woody Clouse*

- When diving for a ball you must determine whether you can hit the ball offensively or defensively. This will depend upon your balance and court position.
- If you are balanced and in good position, go for a winner.
- If you must be defensive, go to the ceiling and regain center-court position.

---

returning your dive shot. See Figure 10.17d where Woody is beginning his recovery phase. Note that he has both hands forward and feet together to make recovery as quick as possible. You need to recover immediately; you cannot lie on the floor and think about what a great return you made. As soon as you have hit the floor and absorbed the impact properly to prevent injury, you must immediately bring your feet under you and use both hands to help bring yourself into a semicrouched position. You can then move quickly toward the return shot by your opponent. Do this as a reflex, without thinking—there is no time. Move to the ball immediately; otherwise the dive was in vain.

Diving Shots

What kinds of shots are possible off the dive? The basic dive return is the ceiling shot. The ceiling shot is the best choice for a number of reasons. First, you are low to start with, and so it is very easy to get under the ball. Second, you need as much time as possible to recover, and the ceiling shot provides it. Third, many of your sources of power are unavailable during the dive, so it's best to use a shot that doesn't require much power.

Occasionally you can dive and hit an offensive shot such as a kill, pass, or pinch. This is difficult, but at times you can catch your opponent off guard with this tactic, especially if he or she is anticipating a ceiling shot.

In any case, keep diving to a minimum, in practice sessions and in game play. We recommend that diving be practiced on a soft, shock absorbing surface such as in foam pits or on extra soft or thick mats.

Occasional diving is fine for advanced-level players. However, if you are diving often, you need to reconsider your playing strategy. No one's body can take the constant abuse of diving. The less you do, the better off you'll be and the less injury and pain you'll endure.

SOUNDS LIKE VICTORY

Two types of sound are important in racquetball; one is grunting and the other is miscellaneous sound in and out of the court. Grunting is the result of applying maximum force. If you are not grunting on hard-hit or hard-to-retrieve shots, you are probably not maximizing your effort. Of course, grunting for the sake of grunting is not really helpful for skill improvement. However, a grunt is a good indicator that you are going all out for the shot, and this is an important aid in winning points.

Listening to the sounds in the court can help improve your game. Other than grunts, the sounds that are important to a player are the sound of feet, the sound of racquet-ball contact, and the sound of ball-wall contact. You should be able to use these sounds to advantage to help you anticipate and react more quickly in a given situation.

For example, if you hear your opponent's feet close behind you while you are in center court, you know that your opponent is moving forward, and you should play a ceiling shot or a passing shot rather than attempt a kill. Also, the sound of a ball coming off a racquet with a crack tells you that the ball has been hit hard. When hit by certain players, kills, passes, and pinches produce different ball-racquet contact sounds. If you can attune yourself to the differences, you can use the sound to anticipate and reach an otherwise unplayable ball.

Also useful is the sound of ball-wall contact. The sound of a crosscourt passing shot may be quite different from that of a pinch, and these differences should enable you to react quickly to the ball. The lack of sound and partial sounds are also important. The lack of sound indicates a touch shot, and partial sound may indicate a spinning ball or a mis-hit shot.

You should also know that balls from different manufacturers make different sounds. You need to get used to the sound of the ball you are using, and this idea carries over to court structure, floor structure, racquet brands, and various string tensions. If you are playing on a court for the first time, hit for a while to get used to the sound. The same is true of new balls, new racquets, or new strings. A newly strung racquet gives not only a different hit but also a different sound.

Background sounds are also important to your racquetball success. This includes sound from adjacent courts, balconies, hallways, and from outside the building. The noise may be from voices, ball hits, yells, scrapes, mowers, or automobiles. You must learn to block out these sounds as you play. Sounds within the court are to be listened to and used to your advantage; external sounds are to be blocked out.

Drills for the Overhead Shot

Self-Toss Drill

Purpose:
To practice setting up overhead passing and kill shots.

Directions:
Stand in the back of the court, toss the ball up high, let it bounce, reach up, and play overhead passing and kill shots (20 repetitions).

Variations:
A. Stand in the back of the court, hit short lobs or short ceiling shots to the front wall, let the ball bounce, and play overhead passing and kill shots.

B. Repeat drills but hit only front-corner kills off the setup.

C. Repeat drills off deep ceiling shots.

Ceiling-Ceiling Overhead Drill

Purpose:
To hit overheads off a ceiling-ceiling rally.

Directions:
Stand in the back of the court and rally the ball with ceiling shots. After hitting a series of ceiling shots, change pace with an overhead passing or kill shot (30 repetitions).

Drill for the Pinch Shot

Drop and Pitch Drill

Purpose:
To practice hitting pinch shots low to a near front corner.

Directions:
Stand near center court but closer to one side wall; drop the ball low and hit pinch shots to the *near* front corner (30 repetitions).

Variations:
A. Use the same drill as above, but drop and hit a reverse pinch to the *far* front corner.

B. Move farther back in the court and drop or toss; hit pinches, reverse pinches, splats, and volley pinches.

Drills for the Wallpaper Shot

Drop and Hit Drill

Purpose:
To practice hitting a ball that hugs the side wall.

Directions:
Stand near a side wall and reach up as high as you can with the ball as close to the side wall as possible. Release the ball so that it drops straight down, wallpapering the side wall. Step back so that you are arm's length from the wall and return the ball with a ceiling shot (25 repetitions).

Front-Wall Toss and Hit Drill

Purpose:

To practice hitting a rebounding ball that hugs a side wall.

Directions:

Stand near a side wall, toss the ball to the front wall so that it rebounds as a wallpaper ball, and return the wallpaper ball with ceiling shots (15 repetitions).

Variations:

A.   Use the same drill but return the wallpaper ball with a wallpaper shot.

B.   Use the same drill but toss the ball with more force to the front wall; allow it to hit the back wall and wallpaper the side wall; play the back-wall wallpaper shot back to the front wall.

Drill for the Around-the-Wall Shot

Self-Toss and Hit Drill

Purpose:

To practice standing in the backcourt and hitting around-the-wall shots.

Directions:

Stand in the forehand rear corner of the court, either bounce or toss the ball up, and hit the around-the-wall shot (20 repetitions).

Variations:

A.   Use the same drill but stand in the backhand corner when you begin the drill.

B.   Use the same drill but vary the speed and height of your around-the-wall balls.

Drills for the Drop Shot

Drop and Hit Drill

Purpose:

To hit a slow setup and to slow it down even more by hitting a drop shot.

Directions:

Stand in center court, bend low, drop the ball low, and hit drop shots into the corner (30 repetitions).

Variations:

A. Stand in the back court and repeat the drill.

B. Use the same drill but vary your technique of dropping from shortened swing, to cutting, to relaxed grip.

Back-Wall Drop Shot Drill

Purpose:
To hit a drop shot off a fast-rebounding back-wall ball close to the front wall.

Directions:
Stand in center court facing the back wall and hit a medium- to slow-speed ball about 10 to 12 feet high on the back wall. The ball will take its first bounce near the service area. Move with the ball toward the front wall and hit a drop shot (30 repetitions).

Variation:
Stand in center court and hit a high, hard shot to the front wall; let the ball hit the back wall in the air and bounce near center court; then attempt to drop it into a front corner by slowing down the forward momentum of the ball.

Drill for the Dive

No drills recommended on the court!

Mat Diving Drill (Partner Needed)

Purpose:
To practice diving on a soft surface to prevent injury.

Directions:
Have a partner throw you a low shot. Begin in a low position, dive onto the mat, hit the ball with a ceiling shot, and immediately recover (15 repetitions).

Part III

COMPETING

Photo by Stan Badz—KILLSHOT magazine

Chapter 11

Covering the Court

*P*rimary factors that differentiate players at different levels are movement patterns and positioning on the court. To cover the court effectively with your feet, you first must be able to cover the court with your brain. Naturally, this chapter will focus on the physical mechanics of court coverage. But we'll give equal weight to the mental aspects. Follow the advice and your footspeed will seem to improve—even though it's your mind that's quicker, not your feet.

GET READY

Before the movement begins, you must be in the basic ready position. Your feet should be about shoulder-width apart, weight forward on the balls of the feet, knees slightly bent, waist slightly bent, and eyes watching the ball or the opponent or both. Hold the racquet either at the body midline or slightly to your backhand side. Be light and bouncy on your feet so that you can move quickly.

Most ready-position descriptions have the player facing forward, but this is accurate only when you are behind the hitter. If you are in front of the hitter, your head should be turned to watch the hitter. The proper ready position gives you the best possible mobility patterns. You can move with ease forward, backward, right, left, or diagonally.

WATCH YOUR OPPONENT

Before moving toward the ball, watch your opponent. Notice where and how the opponent is positioned and, especially, racquet position at ball contact. By carefully watching your opponent's body, feet, and racquet positions, you can determine the type of shot to be played even before the ball is hit. Many players telegraph the shot by the way they set up.

In Figure 11.1 Ed, in the frontcourt, can see Woody getting set for a ceiling return before Woody ever contacts the ball. As soon as the ball leaves your opponent's racquet (or sooner), you can be moving to the area where the ball is going because you will know whether the ball is going deep or short, left or right. As you move you begin to fine-tune your estimate of where the ball is going. As you close in on the ball, it becomes easier to determine the *exact* spot from which to take the optimum shot. As you approach the hitting zone, position yourself for the shot. Ideally, you would like to be able to stop, get set, and hit the ball using the correct skill mechanics and power supply sources.

BE LIGHT ON YOUR FEET

Bounciness or lightness on the feet is a means of keeping your body moving continuously so that you can easily change direction.

Figure 11.1 Watch your opponent so you can anticipate the upcoming shot. Note that Ed is already beginning to move back for the ceiling shot.

Bounciness takes many forms such as shuffling, bouncing, weaving, skipping, sliding, hopping, dancing, or just nondescript moving. You should be in continual motion and never standing still between shots.

Being in motion enables a player to react more quickly to any of the opponent's shots. The moving player can react more effectively to crotch shots, unexpected wall shots, and strange angle shots. Three factors are critical to ready-position movement: first, all movements must be small and controlled; second, your feet must always be close to the ground; and third, you must always be moving on the balls of your feet.

Small, controlled movements maintain balance and coordination. If your movements are too large or too quick, you could lose control of your body, lose balance, and lose time. If you lose balance you cannot easily change direction. If you lose control you may be moving too far or too fast in the wrong direction. If your feet are too far off the floor, it takes too long to obtain the traction to move your body in the desired direction.

You must be on the balls of the feet to be able to move in all directions. If your weight is on your heels, or even distributed between the balls of your feet and heels, you will lose valuable time transferring your weight forward. You may be unable to return a shot that you should have been able to return. All the preliminary movement patterns and skills are designed to help you move quickly so that you can be in the best position to retrieve the ball with power and control.

FOOTWORK

All footwork is designed to put you in the right place at the right time. Court-covering movement is initiated by moving the feet. You can shuffle-step, step out with the lead foot, jab-step with the lead foot, or cross over with the trailing foot. As mentioned in chapter 9, the step-out and crossover steps are the quickest for covering shots far from your starting position. Woody is using a step-out with the lead foot for a forehand in Figure 11.2. If the ball is not too far away, shuffling is the best method of moving because it is easy to stay in control of your body.

You may move in any direction, but the most useful patterns are diagonal movements across court both forwards and backwards.

Figure 11.2   Woody steps out with his lead foot to cover a forehand.

Diagonal movements are the quickest and shortest routes to retrieve the ball. Circular paths and angular paths are not as quick as diagonal movements (see Figure 11.3).

Stay low as you move. Keep your body bent at the knees. You should be in a semicrouched position while moving, just as you were in the initial ready position. From the semicrouched position you can uncoil into the ball and hit with greater power than if you were standing erect.

Controlling your movement will help you return freak shots and will reduce the number of times you misjudge balls. Control the length and speed of your steps. If the ball is far away, initially take large steps to cover as much ground as possible. As you get closer to the ball, shorten your steps to set yourself in an effective hitting position.

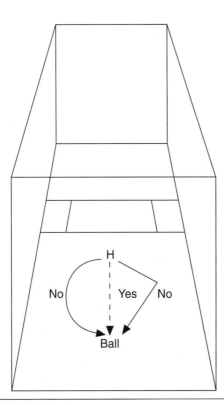

Figure 11.3 The shortest distance to the ball is a straight or diagonal path—not a circular or angular path.

STOP TO GET SET

Imagine shooting a rifle while you are running as opposed to while you are standing still. Of course, you are likely to shoot much better from the stationary position. It's the same in racquetball: Your shooting is much more accurate and consistent when you can set up properly. If you are running and hitting the ball at the same time, your stroke and shot placement will be less effective.

However, when you do not have time to set up properly, two strategies may be helpful. First, think slow motion and swing with less than full power; hit the ball at half or three-quarter speed. Second, play percentages and use a shot that has a good chance of success. These strategies will allow you to hit your best possible shot under difficult circumstances.

CONTROL CENTER COURT

Your movement patterns after any shot, like any serve, should always be in the direction of center court because you can control the game from this position. As shown in Figure 11.4, center court is an oval area 15 feet wide and 8 to 10 feet deep located behind the short line. Your movement patterns away from the ball are just as important as your movement patterns toward the ball. Reaching center court after your shot is as necessary to winning as moving into position to hit. All the elements of proper movement toward the ball apply also to your movement patterns to center court.

ANTICIPATION

Some players will amaze you with their quickness and ability to retrieve apparently unreachable balls. Quickness in body movement is important, but anticipation is also important in successfully retrieving apparently nonreturnable shots.

You can learn to anticipate and thus improve your ability to retrieve balls by using three key concepts. First, analyze your opponent's likes and dislikes. Second, remember which shot is used in a particular situation and where the ball will end up. Third, learn to read the ball and your opponent.

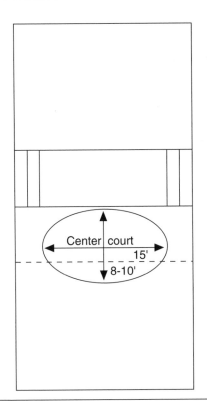

Figure 11.4 Center court—always your goal.

Analyze Your Opponent

Every player prefers to hit certain shots in certain situations. Once you analyze and learn your opponent's preferences and idiosyncrasies, you can anticipate his or her shot in a particular situation. Also, your opponent's skill level may restrict him or her to certain shots in certain situations; if your analysis is correct you will recognize the situation and anticipate the shot. Watching your opponent play other opponents will help your analysis. If this is not possible, observe your opponent's warm-up and analyze his or her strengths, weaknesses, and shot preferences. If you play an opponent often enough, of course, you will have analyzed him or her already and will be able to apply that information to your current match.

When analyzing an opponent, also look for idiosyncrasies such as improper positioning on certain strokes, odd grips, and other unusual aspects. These odd habits cause players to hit in surprising ways that you will be able to anticipate.

Remember Specifics

The second major area of anticipation is remembering. Remembering is different from analysis and takes two forms. First, make mental notes of what your opponent does in a given situation. You are not analyzing specific mechanics; you are remembering only likes and dislikes of your opponent. If you can remember these shots during a game, you can get a jump on retrieving the ball.

Second, remember where the ball will end up considering its speed, spin, angle, and height. There are thousands of ways for a ball to react in the court. The more you play, the more you learn about the bounce of the ball; the more rebounds and angles you can recall, the better you will be able to anticipate where the ball is going to end up.

Read the Ball and the Opponent

Effective anticipation requires you to watch the ball and your opponent as he or she sets up and strikes the ball. If your opponent is behind you, you *must* turn your head to watch. Your opponent's point of contact and subsequent openness or closure of the racquet's face determines the path of the ball. Contact can be even with the front hip, in front of the body, or behind the hitter. You must determine how the contact point will affect the position of the racquet face. Keep in mind this will vary depending on whether your opponent is a lefty or righty and whether he or she is hitting from the forehand or backhand side.

The height of the ball contact is also important. It is easy to play a high ball high and a low ball low, so if your opponent's ball contact is high, look for ceiling shots; if low, look for kills; if waist high, look for passing shots.

Another element to look for is the position of your opponent in the court. If your opponent is deep, most shots will be passes and ceilings; if your opponent is forward, look for kills. On any setup, think kill.

Still another factor that helps in anticipation is reading angles and direction as the ball comes off the wall. A ball traveling straight along and close to a side wall will probably be returned straight back to the front wall. A shot caroming off the side wall has a good chance of being hit back to that side wall.

Reading the opponent also helps anticipation because the way the opponent sets up will often telegraph the shot. If your opponent's feet are pointed directly to a side wall, the shot will probably be a parallel shot. If your opponent's feet are pointed or angled toward the front wall, it will probably be an angled return. If your opponent's hitting shoulder is dropped, look for a lower power shot. If your opponent's hitting shoulder is up, look for a ceiling shot. If your opponent's shoulders are parallel to the front wall, look for a shot with minimum power. Finally, if your opponent is facing the back wall, expect a back-wall—back-wall return.

You react to the ball's spin, speed, height, power, and angle. If you watch the ball and your opponent's positioning for the stroke, you can react much more quickly than if you face the front wall and react to the ball when it comes into your peripheral vision.

Key Elements for Court Coverage

- Use the most efficient movement patterns to get to the ball or to get to center court.

- Always watch the ball and your opponent to anticipate and react more quickly to the ensuing shot.

- Shuffle steps give you the most control over your body while moving; however, if you must move a great distance, step-outs and crossover steps are better.

Taking Your Game to Its Highest Level *Woody Clouse*

- Do not give your opponent too much space in any area of the court. All points on the court should be of equal distance from your position.

- Maintain presence that puts pressure on your opponent. This is achieved by always being ready to retrieve the ball when your opponent is returning your shot.

- Adopt the attitude that any ball is retrievable. This will help you to never quit on any ball.

Drills for Court Coverage

Turn-and-Watch Drill (With Partner)

Purpose:

To learn to watch your opponent and the ball consistently.

Directions:

Rally the ball with a partner and practice constantly watching your partner and the ball by looking forward and by turning your head to look back. (Play five-minute intervals.)

Shuffle and Hit

Purpose:

To practice movement to the ball, stopping and getting set, and hitting the ball effectively.

Directions:

Run 10 feet using the shuffle step. Stop, drop the ball and hit a shot (30 repetitions).

Variations:

Do the same drill using step-outs, jab steps, and crossover steps.

Mini-Court Racquetball

Purpose:

To practice constant shuffle movement.

Directions:

Play this game with an opponent using the area forward of the front service line. All balls are hit slow and all serves are lobs. The ball must stay in the frontcourt area at all times (ten-minute games).

Chapter 12

Outthinking Your Opponent

Photo by Charlie Palek—KILLSHOT magazine

*E*lements of strategy have been mentioned throughout this book, but this chapter will take an in-depth look at various strategies and how you might best use them. Remember that strategies can become more or less important as your skills improve. However, a few basic strategies apply to all players, and these are discussed first.

STRATEGIES FOR ALL

Whether you are an advanced, intermediate, or beginning player, the following strategies will help you improve your play. These five elementary strategies focus on the basic principles of racquetball play. If you've been paying attention, they should sound familiar to you.

1. Control Center Court. As we discussed in the previous chapter, a major strategy for all players is to control center court, the oval 15 feet wide and 8 to 10 feet deep just behind the short line. From this position you have an equal chance of reaching all portions of the court. You will then have offensive rather than defensive shot selection. Fight to stay in this oval on all shots.

2. Hit to Your Opponent's Weakness. Hitting the ball to your opponent's weakness is one of the most important strategies in the game. Generally this means picking on your opponent's backhand. But don't assume this to be the case; at the upper levels of play, the backhand is likely a player's best stroke.

3. Hit Away From Your Opponent. Another almost obvious strategy is to "hit it where they ain't." Hit pinch shots, kills, and drop shots when your opponent is in backcourt and hit passing shots and ceiling shots when your opponent is in center court. Hit to the right side of the court if your opponent is in the left side and vice versa. Constantly keep your opponent on the run and make his or her shots more difficult to execute.

4. Shoot for the Corners. Hit most shots into the back corners, in particular the backhand corner. The corners are the farthest back you can pin your opponent. Returns must travel a greater distance, giving your opponent the greatest opportunity for error. Also, the corners make swinging very difficult. In addition, the strange angles and rebounds that come out of the corners make life more challenging for your opponent.

5. Be Patient and Play the Ball Low. Let the ball drop low rather than rushing and playing it high. The lower you play the ball, the lower it will hit the front wall and the more difficult it will be for your opponent to return. Remember, if you play the ball too low to the floor, your chance for error increases. You want to hit the ball low but within your comfort zone.

The strategies are summed up in Figure 12.1. Remember, these are basic strategies for all levels of play.

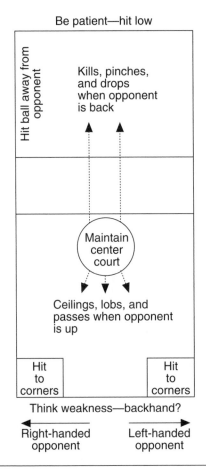

Figure 12.1 Strategies summed up.

ADVANCED SHOT SELECTION STRATEGIES

The remaining strategies in this chapter are based on the skill level of both you and your opponent. Knowing your own and your opponent's levels of skill is an essential part of racquetball strategy. It is also important to understand that strategies can change from match to match, game to game, or even point to point depending on the abilities of the players.

1. Aggressive Shot Selection. The aggressive strategy includes three steps. Step one is to employ the kill, the most offensive shot in the game, whenever possible. If you cannot hit the kill, the second step is to go for the next most offensive shot, the pass. If you cannot kill or pass, go to step three: be defensive and hit the ceiling ball. Thoughtful use of offense is the key to this strategy.

2. Ball Height Strategy. A second general strategy is based on the height of the ball at racquet-ball contact. If you contact the ball at knee level or lower, you kill. If it is contacted between the knee and waist, you hit a passing shot. If you contact the ball above the waist, you go to the ceiling. In this strategy you are selecting the shot with the least chance of error based on the height of the ball.

3. The Two-Shot Strategy. A third strategy you can use is the kill-and-ceiling two-shot strategy. You kill everything except the chest-high or higher ball, which you take to the ceiling. You hit no passing shots, around-the-walls, drops, or other kinds of shots. Kill almost every ball unless it is too high. This strategy, of course, is not very useful for the beginner.

4. Court Position Strategy. A fourth strategy addresses the relative positions of you and your opponent. If your opponent is between you and the front wall and you have a setup, below the waist, you should pass. If your opponent is behind you and you have a setup, you should kill.

5. Serving Strategy. A last strategy for shot selection is based on who is serving. If you are serving, you should always be on offense and take risks by employing offensive shots. In other words, hit kills when serving. However, when you are receiving, hit passes rather than kills and ceilings rather than passes. You should not take risks when receiving. For a summary of shot strategies see Table 12.1.

PLAY YOUR GAME

"Play your game" sounds simple and it would be if you did not have an opponent who was trying to play his or her game. Your strategy

Table 12.1 Summary of Five Advanced Shot Selection Strategies

(1) Aggressive strategy	(2) Ball height strategy	(3) Two-shot strategy	(4) Court position strategy	(5) Serving strategy
Kills first Passing second Ceiling third	Ball contact below knee— kill Ball contact from knee to waist—pass Ball contact above waist—ceiling	Kill everything below chest height Ceiling if chest high or higher	Opponent between you and front wall and the set-up is below the waist—pass Opponent behind you and you have a setup—kill	When serving take risks— hit kills, volleys, pinches, and passes When receiving take no risks—pass first and ceiling second

may collide with your opponent's strategy because of differences in your respective styles of play. You may be unable to impose your strategy or prevent your opponent from executing his or her strategy. This does not mean you should abandon your overall strategy. You must learn to be flexible when parts of your game are not working, and you should be able to subtly adjust these parts. For example, if all of your pinches are coming out high, don't give up on kills; instead try straight, front kills rather than pinches. Making modifications within your strategy is much more effective than changing your entire strategy.

SCOUT AND KNOW YOUR OPPONENT

If you are playing someone you have never played before, you should scout him or her. Look at court speed. Is the player fast or slow on the court? Is the opponent tall, short, left-handed, right-handed? Does he or she have good reflexes? Is the new opponent a shooter or a passer? Is the opponent a control player or a power player? Can the opponent switch gears and change styles of play? Does the player always hit the same shots in a given situation? Does the player telegraph shots? Does your new opponent lose concentration? How does the opponent react under the stress of losing and winning? You should take advantage of your opponent's weakness and play away from his or her strengths, and scouting is an excellent way to learn what you're up against before the match begins.

Try to disrupt your opponent's playing style without disrupting your own. If you are playing a power player, slow the game down. Hit slow, soft, high shots, ceilings, and around-the-wall shots. Hit high, soft serves—Zs and half-speed serves—against the power player. If your opponent is a control player, speed up the game's pace and hit hard, low shots. Shoot and pinch. Use power serves and hard Zs. Hit shots as hard as you can without sacrificing accuracy.

Play your game whenever possible. If you can play a winning power game (your game) over a power player, do so. The same is true if you and your opponent are control players. Play your game and use strength against strength or strength against weakness. You will win more by employing your best strategies and skills. Modify your style only if it is not winning for you. If your style of play is being devastated, you can do no worse by changing tactics, and you just might turn the game around.

PLAYING A LEFTY

If you are right-handed and your opponent is left-handed, prepare yourself mentally before you step in the court. Waiting until you get part way through a game may be too late to make the needed adjustments. Take a look at Figure 12.2. You should immediately note who is left-handed and who is not. You must be able to do this as soon as you step into the court.

Left-handed players have some distinct advantages over right-handed players. First, left-handed hitters are in the minority of players, but the majority of their opponents are right-handed. Thus they are very familiar with right-handed players, but right-handed players are not as used to left-handed players.

A second point to remember is that the elements of play of a left-hander are opposite to those of a right-handed player. For example, the ball has a different spin on it and takes reverse angles out of the

Figure 12.2 Righty Ed needs to change his game. Lefty Woody does not.

corners. To adjust properly, the right-handed player must carefully think through these factors.

Lastly, because almost all players design their strategy to play right-handers, the left-handed player playing a right-handed player does not have to alter his or her style of play. However, right-handed players have to totally change their strategy and style when playing a left-handed player.

If you're a righty playing a lefty, think opposites and be sure you have your strategy ready before you step in the court. Of course, if you're a left-handed player, you can exploit all of these advantages to keep the right-handed hitter off balance. It is a good policy to play a left-handed player in practice matches before you enter tournament matches. Playing the left-handed person is one of the best ways to practice for tournament lefties.

THE MENTAL GAME

Often the physical skills of two players are equal, and yet one player consistently comes out the winner. The reason? The mental aspect of the game. In this section we will discuss various mental and emotional aspects of the game. Racquetball is a game of flows of points, and it is important to keep these flows going for you rather than against you.

Set Positive, Specific Goals

The importance of the motivational goals you use both before and during play cannot be overemphasized. You must set specific goals and they must be positive. If you don't, you really have no game plan, which is like taking a car trip to a new place without having any directions. Furthermore, goals must be focused on *your* behavior, not your opponent's behavior.

A positive, specific goal might be phrased, "I am going to hit 80 percent of my kill shots perfectly." Don't use a negative approach such as, "I will hit only 20 percent of my kills poorly." Think positive about every situation. Avoid general, nonspecific goal statements such as, "I will play well." This is too broad. Tell yourself, "I will hit 95 percent of my ceiling shots to the backhand corner" or "I will control center court 75 percent of the time."

Concentrate

Concentration means focusing your attention completely on the game you are playing as it is being played. Failing to concentrate turns the flow of points to your opponent. To play racquetball effectively, you must be paying attention to a number of factors: watching the ball and your opponent, hitting with proper mechanics, gaining and holding center court, playing your game rather than your opponent's game, playing offensively rather than defensively, and so on. If you are worrying about your last game or your next game or if off-court distractions gain the upper hand, the quality of your play will suffer. But if you can concentrate on the match in progress, you will play at your highest level and the final score will reflect that fact.

If you cannot concentrate totally on the points, games, and match at hand, attempt to take some time-outs to adjust your thinking. Try to concentrate on one simple item such as a number, a word, or a simple figure like a square or a circle. This concept of concentration can eliminate the clutter in your mind and help you concentrate on the game at hand. Experiment with concentration on a range of simple ideas to find which works the best for you.

Play One Point at a Time

Play each point as it comes. Don't be concerned with the midgame or the endgame until you get there, and don't worry about the previous point or the next point—concentrate on the point you're playing as you play it. Moreover, play each point enthusiastically. This makes you feel better about yourself and may cause your opponent to lose concentration. You may be excused for getting physically fatigued, but there is no excuse for mental fatigue or lack of concentration.

If a bad call is made by either your opponent or an official, you need to forget that call and continue to concentrate and play your game. Think and concentrate on the positives of your play, not on the bad call. Use the same philosophy for bad bounces. Again, if it is only one bad bounce, concentrate on the positives of your play, not the bad bounce.

One bad bounce or one bad call should be simple enough for most players to overcome. What do you do when a number of bad bounces or bad calls go against you? First, if the bad calls are being made by an official, you may request a new official. If the bad calls are being made by your opponent, there are different strategies you can employ. You might turn your play up a notch or two to nullify the bad calls. If you cannot turn up your game any further, you should try to discuss the bad calls with your opponent and have the point replayed. If there is no way to discuss the bad calls, you can stop playing this opponent or you can call all close calls your way so that you "balance out" the bad calls your opponent has made. The most important item is to maintain your concentration. Some players do use bad calls to rattle their opponent; you must not allow that to happen. Use the aforementioned concepts to better keep your concentration on bad calls.

Bad bounces are part of the game and you have very little control over them. Normally bad bounces even out over the course of play. Sometimes it seems that every other ball your opponent hits is a bad bounce for you. It could be just bad luck or it could be that your opponent is attempting to hit these bad bounces. If it is luck it will eventually change; if it is skill try to change your game so that your opponent cannot hit all of those bad bounces. Sometimes players get into a groove and you must just wait it out until the groove disappears.

TIME-OUT STRATEGY

Time-outs are strategically important from a number of perspectives. First, if you think you physically need one, call one. Don't play past your limit and risk injury. Also, if you have lost concentration and mental control of the game, call a time-out. Finally, you should call time-out to stop a flow of points being run by your opponent. This is important in today's shorter 11-point games. Many players think that if your opponent runs off four points in a row, a time-out should be called whether you are ahead or behind. You don't want your opponent to sneak through the game and catch up to you or win. Use your time-outs early in the game as well as late, although it is usually a good idea to save at least one time-out for the last part of a game.

When your opponent calls time-out, stay psyched up and spend the time concentrating on your game. In other words, use your opponent's time-out for your benefit. If it helps you, keep hitting the ball when your opponent walks off the court.

When you are receiving service, you are entitled to a ten-second mini time-out if you need a moment to get it together. Raising your racquet tells the server and referee you need your ten seconds. Also, when time is called because the ball breaks, equipment needs repair, or sweat gets on the floor, maintain your concentration; don't let these unforeseen incidents annoy or distract you.

PRACTICE

The importance of practice—by yourself, with a partner, and in game situations—has been mentioned throughout this book. Physical practice can alleviate some of the concentration problems you might encounter when playing. Skill practicing by yourself or with a partner is a form of concentration since repeatedly hitting the same shot requires close attention. We suggest at least one to two hours of skill practice individually or with a partner on a daily basis.

Practicing games with different opponents gives you a chance to react to different personalities on the court. The more that you practice in game situations, the more you will come across good and bad court etiquette by your opponents. This practice helps you to deal with the issues of your opponents' court etiquette and mannerisms.

Key Elements for Strategies

- Maintain center court.
- Hit the ball away from your opponents, not to them.
- Establish your game; do not allow your opponents to establish their type of play.
- Practice both physically and mentally for game situations.
- Practice, practice, practice, and practice some more!

Taking Your Game to Its Highest Level

- Before scouting your opponent, you need to be aware of your weaknesses and strengths. This will help you understand how to attack your opponent's weaknesses while hiding your deficiencies.
- While scouting your opponents, you first need to look for ways to attack and break down your opponent's game. Look for weaknesses that can be exploited that will also feed your strengths.
- Formulate a game plan that will bring out the best of your game. This will always be more comfortable and productive than trying to play a style that really doesn't feel right to you. You will end up playing poorly and then it will seem that nothing feels right for you.

Chapter 13

Playing Tournaments

Photo by Stephanie Secrest—KILLSHOT magazine

*T*ournaments are a different ball game from everyday playing with your friends. You must physically and mentally shift gears when heading into tournament play. This chapter contains a variety of suggestions and information to help you prepare for and play better in tournaments at every level of competition—local club tournaments as well as state, regional, and national-level tournaments.

Win or lose, tournaments can be a lot of fun. Be a good sport, learn from your mistakes, play to win, and accept it when you lose. Remember that racquetball is improving your health both mentally and physically and may help you live a longer, happier life.

Probably the most important characteristic of racquetball players is the desire to win, and today's tournament players face fierce competition at all levels of play. The desire to win can cause some intensely stressful situations that even the most seasoned player has trouble coping with. We believe that competitiveness takes some of the fun out of the game for the person who plays purely for enjoyment and fitness, but it is also the driving force behind the popular success racquetball has attained in such a short time.

Tournament racquetball players are a diverse group of athletes. It is very difficult to describe a clear-cut style of tournament play because under certain situations a well-rounded player will exhibit almost every style of play. This ability to adapt is what makes the best players come out on top.

PREPARING FOR THE TOURNAMENT

Your preparation for any physical endeavor should start many months before the event takes place. Tournament success depends on both how skilled you are and how long you can maintain your skill level. Many excellent players simply run out of gas before they reach the finals because they are not at peak physical condition. Along with many hours of racquetball, you should condition yourself by sprinting, jogging, weight-lifting, and participating in aerobic activity.

Mental Preparation

Mental preparation is also important and is closely linked to physical preparation. It is much easier to plan and execute your strategy if you know you are in shape and physically prepared for the tournament.

Mental preparation before a tournament is complex because your strategy depends on many variables specific to each tournament site. The following items are some of the areas you must consider for tournament preparation.

- **Type of ball**—Some are fast and some are slow.
- **Type of walls**—Some are faster than others; some allow more spin on the ball.
- **Air-conditioning**—Cold courts make the ball slower and warm courts speed up the ball.
- **Glass walls**—Some players have vision problems on glass.
- **Lighting**—If courts are darker, it is more difficult to follow the ball. If courts are brighter, it is easier to follow the ball. Outside court lighting and background are important on glass courts. If outside court lighting is bright, it is easier to follow the ball. Dark carpeting in the background in a glass-walled court makes following the ball more difficult.
- **Food**—Does the tournament provide the type of food you normally eat? If not, you need to bring food with you. You may be able to find a nearby restaurant or grocery store that serves the type of food you normally eat.
- **Host club**—Are locked lockers provided or do you need to bring your own lock? Are towels provided? Does the club provide other amenities such as whirlpools, trainer, and hair dryers?
- **Time**—Be at the club at least one hour ahead of time. Know whether you are playing in the morning, afternoon, or evening and know the day of your first match.
- **Transportation**—Can you drive or will you fly to the tournament? If you fly, you must arrange in advance for your hotel and local transportation to the tournament.
- **Gallery**—Is there a large gallery area? Is the viewing area above, behind, or on the side of your court? You will need to adjust to the gallery location. Will you have support in the viewing gallery from friends or family?
- **First tournament**—Your first tournament will be a learning experience, both physically and, even more so, mentally. You must play in tournaments to develop a "tournament mentality."

These factors vary from tournament to tournament and facility to facility, and they must be considered during your preparation. When you know what to expect, you can adapt your strengths and weaknesses to the situation. You should analyze your game realistically, determine your advantages and disadvantages in terms of the tournament variables, and develop a unique game plan for yourself.

Adequate physical and mental preparation should help make you confident in your ability. This preparation will help you deal with the pressures of the crucial first game, which is when you get rid of the butterflies, see what kind of shape you are in, and try to execute the strategy you have planned.

Warming Up

You should spend a lot of time warming up before the first match. You need to make sure that all of your muscles are loose because with the excitement, tension, and added adrenaline it is very easy to pull a muscle. In most tournaments, when you lose you are finished, and to lose the first round is not only embarrassing but expensive. Do everything you can to win and make it to your second match. Once you survive this ordeal, it will be easier to prepare for the matches that follow. Find out whom you will be playing and get a little rest before the next match. Hitting for practice in the same type of court you're playing in will help you feel more comfortable with your tournament game.

The Calls

Because racquetball is such a fast game, you need to prepare for the questionable calls that will invariably occur. You are going to win some and lose some, and maintaining your concentration through these moments is crucial. An experienced player may intentionally use an emotional outburst to try to ruin your concentration.

THE TOURNAMENT STRUCTURE

Racquetball tournaments are a lot of fun and they should be—you pay anywhere from $15 to $50 as a registration fee to exhibit your skills. What exactly do you get? Upon arrival you are asked to check in, and then you are given a bag of goodies. Depending on the amount of your registration fee, this bag may contain the following: T-shirt, shorts, eye guard, wristbands and headbands, socks, rule book, door-prize tickets, and an assortment of coupons and discount cards from area sponsors for food, equipment, and housing.

During some tournaments, meals are included for players. Most tournaments offer Gatorade, fruit, and even beer, which only the less serious players should drink. The tournament usually sponsors a party and dinner on Saturday night for the players; this occasionally changes the outcome of Sunday's matches.

Certain other practices are common in tournaments. Most tournaments are held on weekends. Early-round play begins on Friday afternoon or evening, and play continues through Sunday. Quarterfinal and semifinal matches are usually played on Saturday. Finals are usually played on Sunday morning. After your match, you will usually referee the next match on your court unless the tournament is large and they provide certified referees.

Divisions

Depending on the type of tournament and court availability, consolation rounds may be held for first-round losers. This guarantees that you play at least two matches. The number and type of events in tournaments vary depending on the number of entrants and court availability. Most tournaments offer open- and A-divisions, B- and C-divisions, and a doubles division or two for both men and women. The larger the tournament, the more events will be available. Large tournaments may have up to 30 divisions differentiated by age, sex, and level of skill. Most amateur tournaments are sponsored by a business as well as the host racquetball facility. Also, most tournaments are sanctioned by the American Amateur Racquetball Association (AARA). To compete, you must pay an entry fee for each event and be a member of the AARA or state ARA. The tournament draw sheets are usually displayed in the main lobby area, and you can usually obtain your starting time a day or two before the tournament by calling the host club. Figure 13.1 shows you a typical large tournament breakdown along with an entry form.

Facilities

Normally, the host facility will open other parts of the club to all tournament participants. You may be able to lift weights, run, or swim indoors; enjoy hot tubs and steam rooms; and relax in the club

Geneva Lakeside Hospital
Benefit
RACQUETBALL
TOURNAMENT

ENTRY FEE: $40 Entry Fee & $5 Referee Surcharge = $45 Open Players
$35 Entry Fee & $5 Referee Surcharge = $40 First Event
$15 Second Event
$15 Juniors

ENTRY DEADLINE: Monday, January 17 at 9:00 p.m.
For phone entries (217)555-3612
Deduct $5.00 if entered/postmarked by January 12.
Phone entries excluded.

MAKE CHECKS PAYABLE TO: Geneva Lakeside Hospital

SEND ENTRIES TO: GLH c/o Geneva Racquet Club
1 Bradshaw Dr., Geneva, OH 44041

STARTING TIMES: Available on Wednesday, January 19
after 5:00 p.m. at (217)555-3612

DIRECTIONS: Route 90 (north or south) to Route 534,
Exit 2 (Fleet Avenue), follow signs to airport.

HOSPITALITY: **Breakfast** will include muffins, donuts, bagels,
(Fri., Sat., Sun.) cereal, yogurt, juice, and coffee.
Lunch & Dinner will include spaghetti, salads, sandwiches,
BBQ chicken, and assorted desserts.
Fruit, pretzels, chips & soda will be available all weekend.

ACCOMMODATIONS: Good Knight Motel. Call (217)555-2020 and mention
the tournament rate of $41/night (up to 4 in a room).

TOURNAMENT DIRECTORS: Geneva Racquet Club and Geneva Lakeside
Hospital

OFFICIAL BALL: Ektelon

RULES:
► All AARA rules apply and AARA membership is required.
► No refunds are given after the entry deadline.
► Consolation matches will be 1 game to 21 points.
► No doubles consolation.
► Divisions must have 12 players to qualify for full prize money.
► Open Divisions will observe the 1-serve rule.
► A 20-minute forfeit time will be enforced for all matches.
► Tournament directors reserve the right to forfeit any player,
without refund, if they are playing in an incorrect division.
► Players must check in 1 hour prior to match time.
► Players *must* be able to play Friday if entering 2 events.
► Anticipation of a large draw may necessitate Friday afternoon play.
► No towels, locks, or babysitting will be provided.

(continued)

ENTRY FORM

Name _____

Address _____

Telephone _(H)_____ (W)_____

DBLS Partner _____

Home Club _____

What time are you available to play Friday? _____

☐ Men's ☐ Women's ☐ Open ☐ A ☐ B ☐ C ☐ D ☐ Novice ☐ Juniors
☐ 30+ ☐ 35+ ☐ 40+ ☐ 45+ ☐ Open Doubles ☐ A Doubles ☐ B/C Doubles
☐ Mixed Open Doubles ☐ A/B Doubles ☐ Mixed B/C Doubles

I hereby, for myself, executors, administrators, or sponsors, waive and release any and all right and claims for damages against Geneva Lakeside Hospital and Geneva Racquet Club for all injuries which may be suffered by me in connection with my participation in this event.

Signature _____
(Parental consent required if under 18)

Figure 13.1   A typical tournament entry announcement and entry form.

bar. If the tournament is too large for one facility, some divisions may play at a different site. For instance, the B- and C-divisions might be played at the local YMCA, and the open- and A-divisions might be played at the host racquetball club.

Prizes

Most tournaments offer money or trophies to first and second place finishers in each division. Many tournaments now offer cash awards up through and including fourth place finishers in each division. Television sets and up to $1,000 are common prizes in the open divisions of sanctioned tournaments. Accepting these prizes does not affect your amateur status.

Referees

Do not be alienated by the term *referee*. Remember that an official is a person first and an official second. The referee is one of three officials found at tournament matches. The tournament director and lines people are the other officials.

The referee may be hired strictly to officiate for the tournament. If the tournament is large enough, referees are paid $5 to $10 for each match. If referees are to be paid, the host facility may offer a short referee clinic before the beginning of the tournament. Usually, however, the referee will be a player from the tournament. The duties of the referee are found in Section III of the AARA Racquetball Rules, so specific responsibilities are not included here. But we will offer some general thoughts about officiating that are important to both the player and the referee.

Know the Rules

If you referee, you need to know all the rules so when you make a call or a call is questioned, you can correctly cite the appropriate rule. Incorrect calls frustrate the players and rattle the referee. So learn the rules and be consistent with your calls. Whether you interpret a rule closely or loosely, call it consistently throughout the match.

Control the Match

The referee must be in control of the match, the players, and some-times the gallery. You must be decisive as well as correct on your calls. You may allow a player to question a call, but you should be able to explain quickly and clearly the reason for the call. If you know beforehand that either or both players harass the officials, take charge. Explain to them that you will not allow any abuse on the court. Arrive at the court early and be organized. Know your respon-sibilities concerning the players, equipment, and scoring. Start the match on time. As the referee you will also be the scorekeeper. Keep score accurately. You should have a pretournament meeting with the tournament director to learn about local hinder calls and other idiosyncrasies of the host club that might affect rule interpretations. If a pretournament meeting was not held, you will need to talk to a local club player and find out the local rules before you officiate.

Lines People

It would also be to your advantage as a referee to appoint two lines people who know the rules and can make decisive calls. When rules are questioned, the two lines people and you should confer and make the final decision according to the official rules.

Like players, some lines people and referees are better than others. Remember that when you question a call. When officiating, do the best that you can.

Key Elements for Playing Tournaments

- Tournament play is much different from everyday play; be sure to prepare both physically and mentally when you enter a tournament.

- The best way to learn about tournament playing is to play in tournaments.

- Plan for your tournament. Know the types of courts you will play on. Bring your type of food with you if it is not provided at the tournament.

- You will probably have to referee during a tournament; make sure that you know the official rules and local rules, that you take charge, and that you are consistent and organized.

Taking Your Game to Its Highest Level

- The number one priority when you enter a tournament is to play for the love of the game. Everything else is secondary. Any other priority will decrease the chances of you playing your best.

- Have a routine to prepare for your competition. A bad routine is better than no routine at all. A good routine will consist of aids that give you an edge.

- Use imagery, stretching, proper diet, proper game plan, and anything else you believe will bring out your best.

*C*hapter *14*

Playing Doubles and Court Games

Photo by Charlie Palek—KILLSHOT magazine

*E*verything we have talked about in this book has dealt with singles. In this chapter we will give you specific advice for playing doubles, cutthroat, and other court games. Doubles and other court games can be more sociable than singles. There are many other aspects of doubles that might appeal to you. You may even find that you prefer doubles to singles.

DOUBLES

Like tennis doubles, racquetball doubles has begun to grow in popularity. A variety of factors have helped the doubles game catch on. Having four people on the court is more friendly and interactive than singles. Doubles is not as physically demanding as singles because you cover only a part of the court. Doubles also challenges you to place your shots more precisely since the openings for winners are fewer.

Some players prefer doubles because they find it faster and more thought-provoking than singles—you must think more to gain smaller advantages. The game can be faster because a partner can cut off the ball, and that gives everyone less time to hit and react. Also, with limited court space available and high court costs (which can be divided four ways), doubles can be more practical than singles.

Doubles safety is worth a special mention. With two more bodies and two more racquets in the court, the increased pace of the game, and more shots in a given time, safety is a substantial concern. Players new to doubles must be very careful to shorten both their backswing and their follow-through. Another major safety principle is to stay out of the way of the other three players and avoid getting hit by the ball. Having a plan of operation for your doubles strategy before entering the court is one method of helping to reduce injuries.

When you want to play serious doubles, you must find a permanent partner who complements your game. Stay with this partner for a year or two to learn to work together as a unit. The workings of a successful doubles team take both mental and physical attributes. You must be able to communicate effectively with your partner on strategies, placements, and skills. You will need verbal and nonverbal communication (such as hand signals).

You will learn, over time, what shot your partner will employ in a particular situation and where your partner will move after such a shot. Each team member will need to give support to the other on both good plays and bad. Positive reinforcement between team members is a must for successful doubles.

Doubles Formations

The two basic formations for doubles are the side-by-side and the up-and-back. These formations may be modified or combined. The formation will determine the playing strategy.

Side-by-Side

The side-by-side formation, as seen in Figure 14.1, divides the court down the middle from front to back, and each player is responsible for half the court. To use this formation effectively, players should be about equal in court coverage and shot ability. If both partners are right-handed, the one with the stronger backhand plays the left side of the court. If partners are left-handed and right-handed, the left-handed player should play the left side of the court.

If players of different ability are partners, the side-by-side formation can be modified slightly. The stronger player handles the left two thirds of the backcourt and left half of the frontcourt. The other partner is responsible for the right half of the frontcourt and the right one third of the backcourt (see Figure 14.2). This variation can be further modified depending on the differences in both coverage and hitting abilities of the partners.

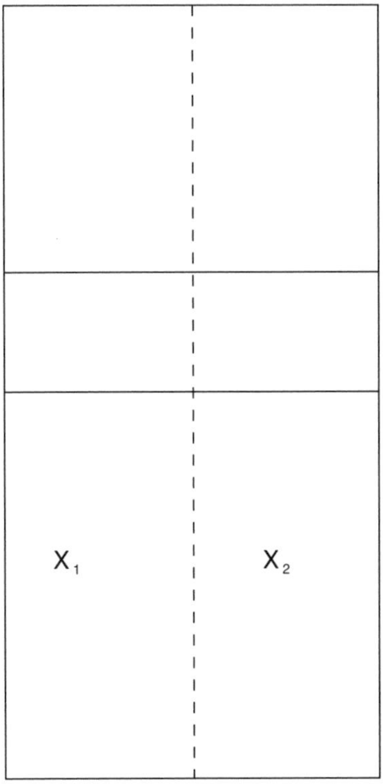

Figure 14.1   The side-by-side formation.

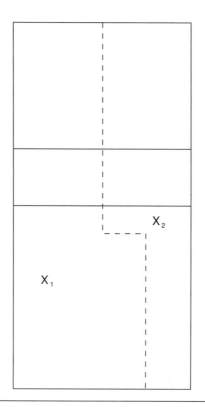

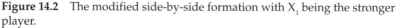

Figure 14.2   The modified side-by-side formation with X_1 being the stronger player.

The right-side player may hit as few as 20 percent of the team's shots in a game, especially if the backcourt is divided by one third to two thirds. Normally, the left-side player decides who takes the shot and gives short commands such as *yours* or *mine*. The left-side player is the leader, and the verbal commands are short because there is so little time to react in doubles.

Up-and-Back

The up-and-back formation, or front-and-back, as seen in Figure 14.3, is rarely used because the partners must have specific skill abilities. The forward player needs to be quicker, more aggressive, and a better retriever than the back player. The back player must be a great deep shooter with an accomplished, well-controlled ceiling game. The up player controls center court while the back player maneuvers from side-to-side to pick up well-placed passing and ceiling shots.

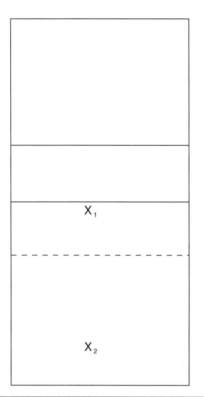

Figure 14.3   The up-and-back formation.

A modification of the up-and-back formation is to stagger slightly from side-to-side while keeping the same basic up-and-back formation coverage. Another modification is for the front player to move further forward and to the right to cover the right front quarter of the court only (see Figure 14.4).

Combination Formation

You must sometimes change your formation during a rally. You may be playing basically side-by-side, but at times you must switch to up-and-back. Both you and your partner should know that the switch has been made and that at the earliest opportunity you will switch back to your usual formation. You might switch from a side-to-side formation to up-and-back when you retrieve a drop shot and are caught out of position in the frontcourt. Your partner assumes the back position while you play up. At the earliest possible time during the rally, you will again move to the side-by-side formation. Com-

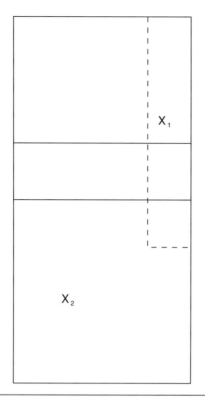

Figure 14.4 The modified up-and-back formation with X_2 being the stronger player.

bination formations are usually dictated by a game situation that forces one or both partners out of their usual position.

A slightly staggered side-by-side position works very effectively in advanced-level doubles play. Both players must have a full repertoire of offensive shots for this formation to work. The staggered side-by-side strategy gives the players the benefits of both the side-by-side and the up-and-back formations.

Doubles Strategy

The skills used in doubles are the same as those used in singles, but doubles play requires some changes in strategies. All shots must be placed precisely in doubles because you have two opponents covering the court rather than one. Shot selection will vary depending upon your opponents' formation. If your opponents are side-by-side, kill shots, pinches, and ceiling shots are effective. If they are in the up-and-back formation, passing shots and pinches work well.

Service

If your opponents are both right-handed, your service strategy is similar to that used in singles. The majority of the serves should go to your opponents' backhand corner. However, if you are playing against left-handed and right-handed opposition, you will probably have two backhands in the middle of the court, and you should direct your serves to the back middle of the court to force a backhand return.

Center Court Control

Controlling center court is a necessity in doubles. Center court gives you better court coverage; your shots should be more accurate because you are closer to the front wall. Holding center court also allows you to be in front of your opponents. You can see the ball more easily, and you do not have to hit around them. You and your partner should constantly play shots to move your opponents out of center court. When you remove them from center court, one of you must take center court.

Communication

Communication must begin before the match. Discuss your verbal and nonverbal cues, coverage patterns, use of time-outs, types of serves, and offensive and defensive shot selection. You should also try to determine your opponents' strategies.

Don't play your opponents' game. If you find this happening, call a time-out and get back into your game plan. If one of your opponents is hot and not missing, don't be intimidated. Work on the other partner. If your court coverage is not working, modify or completely change the coverage pattern. Always position yourself in the most advantageous place to play the next shot even if your partner has just returned the ball.

Key Elements for Doubles

- Communication and compatibility of partners both on and off the court are paramount in the success of a doubles team.
- Apply the strategies appropriate for the type of game you and your partner play best.
- Select a permanent partner and stay together for a year or two.
- Splats, wide-angle passes, and pinches are usually good doubles shots.

Taking Your Game to Its Highest Level   *Woody Clouse*

- Play doubles only with someone you like and respect as a player and as a person. If you don't, you're going to be put in a very uncomfortable position.
- You will win or lose as a team, and it is better to go through victory or defeat with a friend.
- Many times in doubles one player will use the other as a scapegoat after a defeat. This should not happen if your partner is a friend you respect.
- Before stepping on the court, discuss game plans and who will take balls down the middle.
- Once the ball is in play, constant communication is a must to bring out the best in both partners.

Try to isolate your opponents' weaknesses and attack the weaker player or the weak spot in their formation. Concentrate on hitting wide-angle passes, pinches, splats, and ceilings. Kill shots are fine, but they need to be almost perfect roll-outs to get by two opponents. When you can, play the ball on the volley to cut down the time your opponents have to return the ball.

It is important to have a partner who works well with you and vice versa. You may find, however, that even after you play together for a while you are still not communicating successfully. This may be caused by having incompatible styles of play. A new partner for each of you might be the best move.

Practice and Praise

To improve your doubles play, practice together as often as possible each week. Work on your problems from previous matches and work on your strong points. During your matches make sure that you let your partner know how well he or she is playing both overall and on a particular shot. This helps your partner's confidence and may provide a psychological advantage over your opponents.

MIXED DOUBLES

Most of our discussion about doubles applies to mixed doubles. As always, your partner should be of about equal ability so that neither of you becomes frustrated at the skill level of the other. This is a partnership, and the more highly skilled partner should not be taking shots away from a less skilled partner.

In mixed doubles, side-by-side and staggered side-by-side play seem to work best. It's common to assume that the woman is the weaker player, so you should be thinking that every ball is coming her way. The real keys for mixed doubles success are to trust your partner, to learn to work as a team, to complement each other, to be compatible physically, and to think doubles.

CUTTHROAT

Cutthroat is a form of the game that allows three players to compete against one another. This game pits the server as a team against two receivers as a team. Hits are alternated from team to team as in regulation doubles.

When the server loses service he or she rotates either clockwise or counterclockwise and becomes the partner of one of the previous opponents. The other opponent rotates to serve (see Figure 14.5). This sequence of rotation continues until the game is concluded. The server is always playing against the other two players. Each player keeps his or her score, and the game ends when a server reaches game point.

Strategies employed in cutthroat are a combination of singles and doubles techniques. As a member of the doubles team, you employ

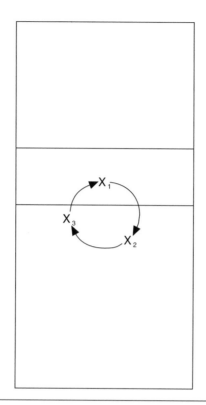

Figure 14.5   Rotation for cutthroat.

singles strategy when playing against the server; as a member of the singles team you employ doubles strategy when serving. Take advantage of weaknesses in either case. Center-court control is paramount to successful cutthroat play. Remember that you are constantly shifting gears from doubles strategies to singles strategies.

COURT GAMES

Racquetball is versatile. Although we have confined our discussion to four-wall indoor play, the game can be played outdoors and on three-wall, two-wall, or even one-wall courts. Racquetball is also played on courts smaller and larger than regulation size and it can be played using two racquets in a sport called Bi Rak Its.

Three-Wall Racquetball

Three-wall racquetball has a front wall and two partial side walls extending back from the front wall anywhere from 1 foot to 25 feet. With no ceiling or back wall, the ceiling shot and back-wall play are gone. The ball is played a little higher than in four-wall courts. The lob replaces the ceiling shot and since it is used often, you have the maximum time to regain your position in the court. Because there is no back wall, many shots must be cut off by playing them on the volley. Three-wall play requires more side-to-side movement and less up-and-back movement than four-wall play.

One-Wall Racquetball

This is similar to the three-wall game, but now the pinch shot and all side-wall shots are eliminated. Angled passing shots work very well because they drive the opponent out of the lined court to retrieve the ball. It is often impossible to run the ball down. Even if a player successfully retrieves the ball, he or she is so far off the court that the opponent can hit an easy winner on the ensuing shot. The long rallies of four-wall play are not found in three-wall and one-wall racquetball.

Two-Wall Racquetball and Modified Courts

Two-wall racquetball is played in a space with a front and back wall or a front wall and one side wall. The wall situation will determine the playing strategies and limits. Courts of modified size are found for one-, two-, and three-wall games. Courts smaller or larger than regulation size are also found in four-wall racquetball. In small four-wall courts the power player with controlled kills is almost unbeatable—the court is simply not long enough for you to force this player out of kill range. Volley shots and ceiling shots are not as effective in small courts, but the back-wall shot becomes the most important shot in the game. If the service zone is placed in front of its regulation distance from the front wall, the power server has a notable advantage because the serve travels less distance and becomes more potent.

In larger-than-regulation courts, ceiling shots, passing shots, and lob serves are the important shots, and the kill and power shots are relegated to the back seat. Some of these odd-size courts were originally squash courts.

Each nonregulation court has distinct strategies and playing patterns. If you are visiting one, all we can do is wish you good luck.

Bi Rak Its

Bi Rak Its is a bilateral developmental sport that can be played in a racquetball court. The court is divided down the center so that the players (each armed with two racquets) use forehands on each side of their bodies; therefore, there are no backhands. Bi Rak Its is played with specially designed racquets that are much smaller than standard racquets to ensure a more controlled style of game. Bi Rak Its helps your footwork, shot selection, and hand-eye coordination. The International Racquetball Tour has adopted Bi Rak Its as its official cross training sport.

Chapter 15

Peak Performance—
Playing in the Pros

*I*n this chapter I'll give you an inside look at what it takes to place your game at the level of a touring pro. Even if you never make the I.R.T., many of the concepts that are included can be adjusted to meet your individual needs to take your game to its highest level.

Woody Clouse

THE I.R.T.

The professional racquetball tour is the goal of any great player. During the International Racquetball Tour's season, you are able to play the best players in the world. This in itself is a way of taking your game to its highest level. To compete at this level, I try to apply all the knowledge I have about myself and racquetball to my game. In short, I try to be faithful and dedicated to my craft.

The I.R.T. is stronger now than it has ever been. There are 25 ranking events held in Canada, throughout the United States, and in Mexico. Corporate America is supporting the pro tour members and ESPN is covering selected pro stops. The racquetball pro tour is definitely on the move and the future looks bright for touring racquetball pros.

A pro stop on the tour is a special tournament for the simple fact that it is an opportunity to prove to the racquetball world that on a given weekend you are the best! Table 15.1 gives you the monetary breakdown of a pro stop. In general, pro stops run in conjunction with amateur events so they are very similar in appearance to any other tournament. But, they are much bigger and they have more media coverage. The media coverage highlights the pros for the most part, but the tournaments are for anyone who plays and loves the game.

Table 15.1   Typical Monetary Placement Breakdown for a $20,000 I.R.T. Event

Round of 32 =	$ 0		
Round of 16 =	200 x 16 =	$3200
Quarterfinals =	700 x 8 =	5600
Semifinals =	1,200 x 4 =	4800
Finals =	2,000 x 1 =	2000
Winner =	3,500 x 1 =	3500
	Total base	= 19,100
Remainder of funding (allocated for various tour costs)		900
Total		$20,000

The pros play much more seriously than other players since it is their job and world ranking points are on the line. But racquetball pros are unique in the sense that they are all there for the love of the game. There are not many prima donnas on the pro tour, and there are not many who play just for the money. I believe that racquetball pros are the best and most underpaid professional athletes in the world.

CLINICS

As a pro, I've participated in the instruction of many clinics. As long as they're well organized, I recommend them. Anytime you have an opportunity to increase your knowledge, it's going to help. This does not mean that clinics are for everybody. Clinics usually don't give you much practice time, nor do they supply you with a lot of one-on-one instruction with the chance to go through repetitive actions (for that I would suggest private lessons). But, if you're a person who can absorb information without having much practice time, clinics are the best way to learn. Not all clinics are held by the touring pros; however, there are some guidelines that will help you determine if a specific clinic will be beneficial to you and your game.

• **Is there more than one person teaching the clinic?** The more high-quality instruction (and the lower the student/teacher ratio) the better, I say.

• **What is the credibility of the instructors?** What type of background and training do they have? There are too many instructors out there who were self-taught. They may claim to be experts but they could lack proper knowledge of racquetball skills and competition.

• **Is the clinic going to be broken down by level of play?** It is always better to teach and learn with people who play at the same level. An A-player and a C-player have separate needs that should be met individually.

• **Does the clinic include video analysis?** Seeing yourself in action is vital to benefiting from a clinic. This will allow the instructor to pinpoint your strengths and weaknesses.

• **Is the clinic scheduled with enough time for the instructors to be thorough?** Three to four hours is the minimum time for a clinic. Anything less may be just enough to confuse you.

WHAT IT TAKES TO BE A TOURING PRO

There are a number of factors needed to make it on the pro tour. The foremost ingredient for a touring pro is love of the game. If you do not love the game, you will never become a touring pro. The following items, not listed in any particular order, are all important to becoming a touring pro on the I.R.T. Physical talent is abundant on the tour and talent is necessary to compete. You must also have financial backing. With twenty or so tournaments a year, travel expenses are between $15,000 and $20,000. (See Table 15.2 for costs of a typical pro stop.)

I feel a will to succeed must be present to do well on the pro tour. Competing against the best players in the world is not easy and defeats are inevitable. Your will to succeed must be able to carry you after a defeat. Just getting to the I.R.T. takes much persistence and time. You must be totally committed to playing the game. You cannot be half-hearted in this attempt to be your best.

Last, but not least, you must be lucky. Anyone who can make a living from playing a game has got to be lucky.

Table 15.2   Typical Costs for a Pro Stop Tour Tournament

Air fare	Average $	350
Entry fee		60
Hotel (5 nights @ $50 per night)		250
Food (5 days @ $40 per day)		200
Entertainment (movies, books, miscellaneous)		100
Rental car or taxi		100
Total expense for a tournament		$1,060

Training

I vary my workout program from day to day to help keep my interest and intensity high. A typical day's workout routine would consist of 15 minutes on the rowing machine, 10 minutes on a stair climber, 15 minutes of stretching, and 20 minutes of footwork speed drills on the court. I also hit drills of 500-1,000 practice balls each day in the court. That's me in Figure 15.1 hitting ball 762 of the day. Usually I am alone for these practice sessions. I lift weights for one hour and swim for 15 minutes each day. I also practice and play with a partner two days per week. Lastly, each day I spend 20 minutes of quiet time using positive visualization. In this technique I actually see myself hit correct shots and winners.

I always make sure that I get a lot of rest so that my body has time to recuperate from such an intensive training and playing program. I stretch each day to keep my muscles loose, responsive, and injury free. Training is the best method of preventing injury while on the tour.

Injuries are a part of sports. Anytime I constantly push my body to the limit, I will experience some injuries from time to time. The best

Figure 15.1   Hitting 500-1,000 balls, alone in the court.

method to stay injury free is to take all the preventive measures possible. If I have an area of my body that is susceptible to injury, it is good to ice this area down after playing. This is a great preventive method to stop injuries from occurring or reoccurring in this susceptible area of my body.

I have also used massage therapy to help my body recuperate from minor injuries more quickly. Obtaining the proper amount of sleep is important in keeping myself injury free.

It is my belief that either you are constantly improving or you are not dedicated enough to your sport. There is no staying the same; it is improvement or nothing. Winning and progress are due to, and are a result of, hard work and determination. Whenever I have the time to train in the off-season or in between pro stops, that is exactly what I do. I believe that you are as strong as your weakest link; therefore, you should work to eliminate your weaknesses.

I try to adhere to the concept of training all aspects of my game off the court as well as on the court. I feel it is easier to do well on the court if you stay well off the court.

There is really not a set formula for racquetball success, but for me it is hard work. In fact, I enjoy the hard work so much that it does not feel like work at all. This dedication and enjoyment of hard work come from my love of the game.

Diet

The old saying "you are what you eat" holds true for playing on the I.R.T. Although I am not a nutrition expert, I have learned about eating well by paying attention to my body's needs during training and competition.

The first and most important dietary habit is to drink an abundance of water. Without water your body is simply not going to function properly while training and competing at the pro level.

I adhere to a high-carbohydrate, low-fat diet. I include many fruits and vegetables along with whole grains and simply cut out all junk foods. I also do not eat foods high in fat and I try to eat an adequate amount of protein to help maintain my muscle mass.

I always eat at least three hours before a match. If my match is delayed I will usually eat a high-carbohydrate power bar that helps me to maintain my energy level. For me, eating four to six small meals a day is better than eating three large meals per day. This makes me feel more energetic and less "weighted down." The most important item for me, concerning diet, is to listen to my body and feed it what it is asking for. If you are going to drastically change your diet, you should consult a nutritionist before you do. I eat well at all times and try to follow a well-balanced diet that excludes foods that are not good for me.

Support

To be on the pro tour you must have a support network. That network includes monetary support and physical and mental support, along with spousal support.

Trainers

Many, but not all, of the pros on the I.R.T. have trainers. Like anything else in this world, there are good and bad trainers. I would not recommend having a trainer just for the sake of having a trainer. If you can find a trainer whom you like and believe in, he or she can be helpful to your game. Trainers can also be helpful in keeping your motivation level high. I have had the opportunity to work with some great trainers and I believe that their knowledge and ideas were very beneficial to me. When looking for a trainer, check the individual's educational background and references. It sometimes helps to call another athlete whom you respect to get an opinion on the trainer. A trainer should make your workouts fun.

Sport Psychologists

With the abundance of talent on the I.R.T., any edge I can achieve, either physical or mental, is something that I should take advantage of. Many individuals feel that to reach the pinnacle of performance at the pro level, you must reach it mentally. Many players who fail to reach their peak have not worked on the mental aspects of the game. A sport psychologist helps me to simplify items that sometimes seem to be confusing. Racquetball is a simple game and my focus, as a player, is to keep it simple. The sport psychologist can help the athlete focus better on skills and game play. This helps to bring out the best in the athlete. I have been fortunate to have a very good sport psychologist who has helped me improve my game. This increased success is why I believe in the use of a sport psychologist.

I practically eat, breath, and sleep racquetball during preparation for a pro stop tournament. With so much time and effort dedicated to my sport, it is also important for me to pay constant attention to my motivational level to prevent burning out.

Sponsors

Pro tour racquetball players must have sponsors to meet the financial obligations of the tour. Sponsors in racquetball are much like employers in the business world. When applying for a position, you have to establish your value to the company and your commitment to your job. I think it is necessary to believe in the companies that you represent. People have an easy time seeing through someone who is not sincere about a product or company that sponsors them. I have been extremely fortunate that all the companies I represent are the best the game has to offer. I suggest that you never accept a sponsor's offer if you do not believe they are the best in the industry. I believe in my sponsors and that is the relationship that should exist between the sponsor and the sponsoree.

Spousal Support

My wife is my best friend. If she weren't, we probably wouldn't be married. The demands of my travel schedule are immense, and having a solid home base to supply balance and support is the most important part of my life. Jacqueline, my wife, is the foundation that allows me to continue to pursue my goals. Her strength and patience are endless. The sacrifices she makes are high and the income I make is low; it takes a special person to stand behind and to support a professional racquetball player. Jacqueline has made this commitment with a sense of class and dignity that is unimaginable. For this I owe her a 100% commitment to do my best on the tour. Without her, my losses would feel much worse and my victories would not be as sweet.

Appendix A

Mini Clinic:
Correcting the 13 Most Common Errors

Sometimes your game falls apart. Your well-honed strokes just disappear. Who knows how or why? In cases like this, you need to diagnose the problem, find the cure, and drill your strokes so you get back into the correct groove. The purpose of this mini clinic is to consolidate into one unit the most basic errors found among racquetball players, to illustrate these errors, and to offer specific suggestions for correcting them.

THE TOP THIRTEEN ERRORS
AND HOW TO CORRECT THEM

Error 1.   *Playing the ball too high.* Playing the ball too high often results from impatience and hitting the ball too soon. This problem causes awkward swings because too little time is available to the hitter. Playing the ball high also keeps the ball high on the front wall.

Correction: Wait for the ball to get low and hit the ball sidearm or underhand, not overhand. When practicing, let the ball bounce a number of times, rather than just once, before you swing. This will give you ample time to get set and will also allow the ball to be bouncing low when you swing. *Be patient and play the ball low.*

See also
pages
76-77.

Error 2.   *Hitting without power.* Improper body position and failure to use all the power supply sources can cause a lack of power.

See also pages 61-67.

Correction: Make sure you are facing a side wall on all shots. If you are facing the front wall, you cannot employ all of your power sources. You should check for a good backswing, good follow-through, stepping into the ball, upper body rotation, and wrist rotation-flexion. The legs should extend into the shot, and both the shoulder and the elbow should help as you contact the ball. All of these forces must be concentrated at racquet-ball impact, and the correct point of contact is approximately opposite the lead foot. Remember the body starts the motion and pulls the racquet around.

Error 3.   *Bending improperly.* Without properly bending, you will have great difficulty keeping your shots low. Bending at the waist (see Figure A.1) prevents you from achieving a low enough body position and impedes your power.

Figure A.1   *Error 3:* Bending at the waist results in high shots and loss of power.

Correction: You must bend at the knees (see Figure A.2). The knee flexion allows you to get very low. However, you can achieve a lower position by also lunging slightly, which gives a good base of support, lowers your center of gravity, and allows you to easily extend your legs into the shot.

See also pages 94-95.

Figure A.2 *Correction 3:* To get down low, bend your knees.

Error 4.   *Hitting balls to midcourt.* Hitting balls at the improper angle (see Figure A.3) or too hard can cause this error, which gives the opponent an easy opportunity for an offensive rather than defensive return.

Correction: If your shot is going to midcourt off the side walls, adjust your shot angle to the front wall. If the ball is going to midcourt off the back wall, hit the ball lower to the front wall or hit with a little less power. If the ball is going to midcourt off the front wall, change your shot angle to the front wall and hit the ball lower on the front wall.

See also pages 70-75.

Error 5.   *Not maintaining center-court position.* This causes you to lose the control and tempo of the game and makes you a defensive player rather than an offensive player. To play effectively, you need to be constantly moving toward center court.

Correction: On returns you should attempt either to win the point or to maneuver your opponent out of center

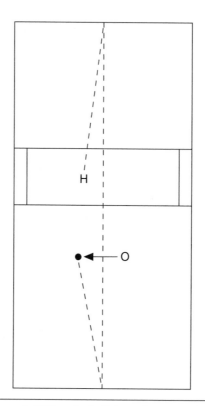

Figure A.3 *Error 4:* Hitting the ball to center court gives your opponent too many easy setups.

court so that you can move into center court. Remember, center court is the oval 15 feet wide and 8 to 10 feet deep directly behind the short service area. You must hit the correct shot at the right time to move your opponent. Use ceiling and passing shots when your opponent is forward. Use kills, pinches, and drops when your opponent is back. Figure A.4 shows Woody in center court just completing a crosscourt pass. Ed must now move to the opposite side of the court and hit a ceiling shot or down-the-wall pass to move Woody out of center court

See also pages 144-146.

Error 6. *Chasing the ball.* If you are constantly running around the court chasing down balls, you will be awkward, tired, and unable to have time to get set for your shot.

Figure A.4 *Correction 5:* Woody controlling center court.

Correction: You must learn to judge where the ball will end up and then move to that position. Running a straight line to where the ball will bounce is always more economical than taking the scenic route around the court.

See also pages 201-205.

Error 7. *Not playing the angles correctly.* Failing to understand rebound angles will prevent you from hitting many shots successfully. You must learn how a ball is going to rebound both off the walls and off your racquet face.

Correction: The racquet face angle should be flat. If the face is too open, the ball will go high. If the face is too closed, the ball will go low. The same is true if you play a ball sidearm or underhand. For the forehand, when the face is angled back, the ball will go off to your right, and if the face is angled forward, the ball will angle off to your left (for the right-handed hitter). For maximum ball control and accuracy, practice keeping the racquet face flat.

See also pages 185-186.

To understand wall angles, you must practice with different speeds and differently angled shots and watch where the ball goes. Use both drills and practice games.

Error 8.   *Hitting with power but without accuracy.* A beginning player who is a hard hitter can win many games by overpowering his or her opponents. But power without accuracy is quite ineffective against a more highly skilled player who has patience, waits for the ball to set up, and then returns it for a winner.

Correction: You may need to sacrifice some of your power to improve your accuracy, but you should not radically change your swing or abandon the power sources of proper hitting mechanics. For example, don't stop your follow-through or shorten your backswing. Instead, try slowing down while maintaining good stroke mechanics. See if your accuracy improves by practicing your stroke at three-quarter speed or halfspeed, or by hitting in slow motion.

> See also pages 121-123.

Error 9.   *Running around your backhand.* Some players think, "Avoid the backhand at all costs because it is my weakness." If you are hitting too many back-wall—back-wall shots, it is because you are attempting *not* to use your backhand.

Correction: Remember that the backhand is an anatomically easy stroke to hit; the problem is we don't use it enough. Therefore, think backhand on every possible shot to get as much practice as possible. This will help you become more familiar with the backhand and more comfortable using it. Take balls out of the backhand corner with backhand shots, try serving with your backhand, and try making all hits with backhands when practicing.

> See also pages 74-75.

Error 10.   *Missing the ball.* This is caused by awkward play and is the result of the many problems already mentioned.

Correction: Use the side-facing basic hitting position (as shown in Figure A.5), anticipate where the ball will end up, and stress accuracy rather than speed. Be patient, learn court geometry, and follow the ball with your eyes, not your body. Your eyes should never lose contact with the ball during a rally.

> See also pages 61-63.

Error 11.   *Constantly skipping the ball.* If you play the ball too far behind the body plane on low passing shots and kill shots, you will naturally rotate the forearm forward. This

Figure A.5 *Correction 10:* A good side-facing-position hit. Notice how Woody keeps his eye on the ball.

closes your racquet face and causes the ball to be angled down. If you attempt to hit the ball too far behind the body plane, you will hurt your elbow if you do not rotate the forearm forward. To avoid hurting yourself, you automatically rotate the forearm forward, which closes the racquet face and skips the ball.

See also page 78. *Correction:* Don't change your racquet face angle. Instead, play the ball more forward, approximately off the lead foot, not behind the body plane.

Error 12. *Using a pushing action rather than a pulling action on the ball.* If you bend over at the waist, you decrease your power supply and will never be able to hit with maximum force (see Figure A.6).

Correction: Lower your center of gravity by bending the knees and rotating the upper body on your pelvic girdle. The upper body rotation is the major source of the pulling action for your arm and racquet (see Figure A.7).

See also pages 64-67.

Error 13. *Hitting from awkward positions, constantly reaching for the ball, and overexaggerating your racquetball motions* (see Figure A.8 for example). When you reach for

Figure A.6   *Error 12:* Bending your waist and pushing the ball result in loss of power.

Figure A.7   *Correction 12:* Here Woody bends his knees and rotates his body to get the pulling action needed for a powerful drive.

Figure A.8 *Error 13:* Hitting outside your comfort zone robs your shots of force because you spend too much energy just reaching for the ball.

balls outside your comfort zone, you expend much energy just meeting the ball.

Correction: All players have their comfort zones as to hitting and movement patterns. Stay within your comfort zone in order to maneuver well and to hit your best shots (see Figure A.9).

See also pages 51-55.

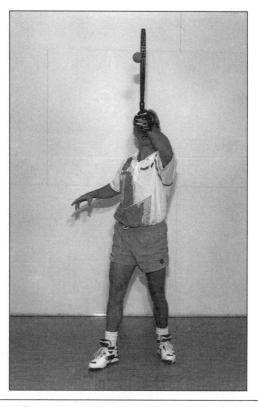

Figure A.9 *Correction 13:* Hitting within your comfort zone allows you to put more energy into the shot.

Appendix B

ADDITIONAL RESOURCES

Books

Adams, Lynn. (1991). *Racquetball today*. St. Paul, MN: West Publishing.

Allsen, P.E., & Witbeck, A.R. (1992). *Racquetball*. Dubuque, IA: Wm. C. Brown.

Collins, D.R., Hodges, P.B., & Marshall, M. (1983). *The art and science of racquetball*. Bloomington, IN: Tichenor.

Edwards, L. (1992). *Racquetball*. Scottsdale, AZ: Gorsuch Scarisbrick.

Isaacs, L. & Lumpkin & Schroder. (1992). *Racquetball everyone*. Winston-Salem, NC: Hunter Textbooks.

Kittleson, S. (1992). *Racquetball steps to success*. Champaign, IL: Human Kinetics.

Norton, C., & Bryan, J. (1991). *Beginning racquetball*. Englewood, CO: Morton.

Stafford, R. (1990). *Racquetball: The sport for everyone*. Memphis: Stafford.

Periodicals

KILLSHOT. Issued five times per year. P.O. Box 8036, Paducah, KY 42002-8036. Tel: 502-441-7723.

Racquetball Magazine. Semi-monthly publication of American Amateur Racquetball Association (AARA). 1685 West Uintah, Colorado Springs, CO 80904-2921. Tel: 719-635-5396. FAX: 719-635-0685.

Racquetball Organizations

American Amateur Racquetball Association (AARA). 1685 W. Uintah, Colorado Springs, CO 80904-2921. Tel: 719-635-5396. The national governing body for racquetball in the United States.

BiRakIts. 5049 Riverpoint Rd., Jacksonville, FL 32207. Tel: 904-398-5428. National office for Bi Rak Its.

International Racquetball Tour (I.R.T.) 13939 N.W. Cornell Rd., Portland, OR 97229. Tel: 530-639-3410. The racquetball organization for professional men players.

Women's Professional Racquetball Association (WPRA). 11355 Affinity Court, #189, San Diego, CA 92131. Tel: 619-536-2393. The organization for professional women racquetball players.

RACQUETBALL EQUIPMENT SOURCES

Ashaway, 24 Laural St., Ashaway, RI. Tel: 800-556-7260.

Champion Glove Company, 2200 E. Ovid, Des Moines, IA 50313. Tel: 515-265-2551. FAX: 515-265-7210.

E-Force, 10366 Roselle St., Suite-A, San Diego, CA 92121. Tel: 1-800-4EFORCE.

Ektelon, 1 Sports System Plaza, Bordentown, NJ 08505. Tel: 609-291-5800.

ESTCA/ESTUSA, 17720 N.E. 65th St., Redmond, WA 98052. Tel: 206-881-8989. FAX: 206-885-4354.

Forten Strings, 12320 Stowe Dr., Poway, CA 92064. Tel: 800-722-5588.

Leader, 675 N. Margaret St., #14, Plattsburgh, NY 12901. Tel: 518-562-1819.

Marty Hogan Racquetball, A Division of Pro-Kennex, 9606 Kearny Villa Rd., San Diego, CA 92126. Tel: 619-271-8390. FAX: 619-566-3686.

Neumann Tackified Glove Co., 300 Observer Dr., Hoboken, NJ 07030. Tel: 201-792-1033.

Penn Athletic Products, 306 S. 45th Ave., Phoenix, AZ 85043. Tel: 602-269-1492.

Power Athletic Footwear, One Silver Court, Springfield, NJ 07081. Tel: 800-437-2526.

Saranac Glove Co., 1201 Main St., Green Bay, WI 54301. Tel: 414-435-3737.

Spalding, 425 Meadow St., P.O. Box 901, Chicopee, MA 01021. Tel: 413-536-1200.

Transition, 1255 Castleton Road North, Columbus, OH 43220. Tel: 800-473-4425.

Wilson Sporting Goods, 7670 Trade St., Ste. 7-A, San Diego, CA 92126. Tel: 619-586-1007 or (in Chicago) 312-714-6800. FAX: 312-714-4590.

Glossary

AARA. American Amateur Racquetball Association. The governing body for amateur racquetball in the United States.

ace. A legal serve that eludes the receiver and results in a point for the server.

alley. The area on both sides of the court near the side walls that is formed by extending an imaginary line from the doubles service box to the front and rear walls.

angle serve. A power serve that first strikes the front wall at an angle and then bounces low to the floor in the safety zone and goes to the opposite back corner.

around-the-wall shot. A defensive shot that strikes three walls—the side wall, the front wall, and then the other side wall—before hitting the floor.

avoidable hinder. An intentional interference with an opponent's shot.

backspin. The reverse or backward rotation of the ball. Also called bottom spin.

backswing. The part of the stroke in which the racquet is brought back behind the body in preparation for hitting the ball.

back-wall—back-wall shot. Ball that is played off back wall and driven back into the back wall and travels on the fly to the front wall.

back-wall shot. Ball that is played off the back wall and driven on the fly to the front wall.

base. The butt end of the racquet handle.

block. The act of preventing your opponent from hitting the ball by using some part of your body.

butt. The enlarged bottom end of the racquet handle.

ceiling serve. A fault serve that contacts the ceiling after hitting the front wall.

ceiling shot. A shot that hits the ceiling of the court before striking the front wall. The ball then bounces off the floor in a high arc to a spot deep in the backcourt. See **reverse ceiling shot.**

center court. An oval area in the middle of the court about 15 feet wide and 8 to 10 feet deep.

continental grip. A one-grip system for holding the racquet. The hand position is somewhere between the eastern forehand and the eastern backhand grips.

control player. A player who relies primarily on shot placement rather than on the force (power) of shots.

corner kill shot. A kill shot that strikes the front wall first and the side wall second.

court hinder. Any obstacle on the court that deflects the ball and interferes with play, such as a door latch, transoms, thermostat, and so forth.

crosscourt shot. A shot hit diagonally from one side of the court to the other.

crotch ball. A ball that strikes the juncture where two playing surfaces meet.

crotch serve. A serve that hits the juncture of the front wall and the floor, side wall, or ceiling. It results in a loss of serve.

crowding. Standing or playing unreasonably close to your opponent.

cutthroat. Game involving three players; each one serves in turn and plays against the other two.

dead ball. A ball no longer in play.

dead-ball hinder. An unintentional hinder resulting in a replay of the point.

dead-ball serve. An illegal serve that is replayed. It does not result in a penalty to the server or the receiver, nor does it cancel any previous illegal serve.

default. The failure of a player or team to compete in a contest because of injury, illness, and so on. It results in an automatic win for the opponent.

defective serve. Any illegal serve—dead ball, fault, or out serve.

defensive position. The back area of the racquetball court. The position assumed to return an opponent's shots.

diagonal formation. A method of doubles play in which court coverage and responsibilities are assigned by dividing the court diagonally from the left front corner to the right rear corner.

dig. To make a good return of a difficult shot that might ordinarily have been a winner.

down-the-wall shot. A shot hit parallel to and near the side wall. Also called a wallpaper shot or down-the-line shot.

drive serve. See **power serve.**

drive service zones. Two lines three feet from the side walls within the service zone. You may not drive serve in the zone you are closest to unless the ball, the racquet, and your body are outside the three-feet area.

drive shot. A hard-hit ball. Also see **passing shot**.

drop shot. A finesse shot hit with little speed and designed to barely reach the front wall.

face. The hitting surface of the racquet; the plane formed by the racquet strings.

fault. An infraction of the service rule.

fault serves. Any two serves in succession which result in a loss of serve.

fly kill. A kill shot that is executed while the ball is still in the air after rebounding from the front wall and before it bounces on the floor.

follow-through. The continuation of the swing after the ball has been contacted. It lends control and direction to the shot.

foot fault. An illegal position of the server's feet during the serve.

forehand. The stroke made with the palm of the hand turned in the direction of the movement of the racquet.

front-wall—side-wall kill shot. A kill shot that hits the front wall first and then the side wall.

garbage serve. A half-speed serve that hits midway up on the front wall and returns to the receiver about shoulder height in either of the rear court corners.

half-lob serve. Same as **garbage serve**.

half-volley. The act of hitting the ball immediately after it bounces on the floor.

handout. Loss of serve by the first partner of the doubles team.

head. The oval-, rectangular-, or teardrop-shaped part of the racquet that contains the strings.

hinder. Interfering with a player during a rally or serve.

International Racquetball Tour (I.R.T). The touring professional organization for men.

kill shot. The act of hitting the ball so low on the front wall that it is practically impossible for your opponent to make a return.

lines people. The referee's two aides who are called upon to judge an appeal call made by one of the players.

live ball. A ball in play or one that bounces exceptionally high.

lob. Similar to the lob serve except that it is hit during a rally. In today's fast-paced game the lob is not often used.

lob serve. A serve hit high and softly to the front wall that rebounds in a high arc towards the back wall.

long serve. A fault serve that rebounds from the front wall to the back wall without hitting the floor.

midcourt. The area of the court between the service line and the receiving line.

midsize racquet. A racquet with 80 to 89 square inches of string surface.

no-man's-land. Area in the court where you do not want to be in relation to the ball and the opponent.

non-front-wall serve. An illegally served ball that strikes any surface of the court before hitting the front wall.

offensive position. Center-court position, the most desirable spot for offensive play. Same as advantage or percentage position.

one-on-two. Game with three players in which the server plays the other two for the entirety of the game.

one-serve rule. A rule in open and pro tournaments that allows the server one serve rather than two.

open face. The angle of racquet-ball contact in which the hitting surface is slanted toward the ceiling; this causes unwanted slicing or backspin on the ball.

out. Failure to return a ball during play.

out-of-court serve. A fault serve in which a legally served ball travels out of the court area.

out-of-order serve. When either partner in doubles serves in the wrong rotation.

out serve. Any serve that results in a loss of serve.

overhead shot. A shot made during a rally by hitting the ball when it is in the air above your shoulder.

oversized racquet. A racquet with 90 to 100+ square inches of string surface.

passing shot. A shot hit near the side wall and out of reach of your opponent.

pinch shot. A kill shot that strikes the side wall first and then the front wall.

point-of-contact. The point where the racquet meets the ball during the stroke.

power player. A player who relies primarily on hitting the ball hard. The player may or may not emphasize accuracy and finesse.

power serve. A serve that is hit low and hard to a rear corner of the court. Also called a drive serve.

rally. The continuing exchange of shots that occurs between the serve and the failure to legally return a shot.

ready position. The body position or stance a player assumes while waiting to make a return of the serve or a shot during play.

receiving line. The short, red dotted line on the floor or side wall five feet behind the short line of the service box.

receiving zone. The area of the racquetball court that extends from the rear wall to the receiving line.

referee. The individual who officiates the match.

rest period. The intervals of rest during and between games taken according to the rules.

reverse ceiling shot. A ceiling shot in which the ball hits the front wall before it hits the ceiling.

roll-out. A kill shot that is hit so low that it rolls on the floor after rebounding from the front wall. This shot cannot be returned.

rotation formation. A system of doubles play in which the methods of doubles strategy and position are determined by the flow of the rally.

safety zone. The area between the receiving line and the short line.

screen ball. A ball that passes so close to a player during a rally or serve that the view of the returning side is obstructed.

service box. The area on either side of the service zone in which the nonserving partner of the doubles team must stand until a legal serve is made.

service line. The line parallel to and five feet in front of the short line; this is the front line of the service zone.

service zone. The area between and including the service and short lines.

setup. A weak return of a shot that results in an easy opportunity for a player to hit the ball for a winner.

short line. The line midway between and parallel to the front and back walls; this is the back line of the service zone.

short serve. A serve that rebounds from the front wall and strikes the floor on, or in front of, the short line.

side-by-side formation. A system of doubles play in which court coverage and responsibilities are assigned by dividing the racquetball court in half from the front wall to the back wall.

side out. The loss of serve by a player or team.

side-wall—front-wall kill shot. See **pinch shot.**

skip ball. A ball that strikes the floor before hitting the front wall.

splat. A shot that hits the side wall close to the hitter and then hits the front wall for a winner.

straight kill shot. A low shot that goes directly to, and rebounds from, the front wall in approximately the same direction from which it came.

tension. The amount of pressure with which a racquet is strung.

thong. The rope or strap attached to the bottom of the handle of the racquet and worn around a player's wrist.

three-wall serve. A fault serve in which the ball strikes three walls in succession before bouncing on the floor.

three-wall shot. See **Z ball**.

throat. The part of the racquet where the handle meets the head.

tiebreaker. The third game of a match, usually played to 11 points.

time-out. A rest period when play stops. Each player is allowed three per game and two in a tiebreaker. The length is usually 30 seconds.

topspin. The forward rotation of the ball that causes it to travel downward and pick up speed after bouncing off the floor.

two-handed backhand. A backhand shot hit using two hands, one above the other, in two forehand grips on the handle.

up-and-back. A system of positioning in doubles play in which one player lines up in front of the other; the forward player covers the frontcourt area and the other player covers the backcourt area.

volley. A ball hit before it bounces on the floor.

wallpaper shot. A ball that hugs the side wall as it travels to the rear area of the court; this shot is difficult to return.

Z ball. A defensive shot that strikes three walls before touching the floor. The ball strikes the front wall, a side wall, and then the opposite side wall.

Z serve. A legally served ball in which the front wall is hit, then a side wall, followed by the ball bouncing on the floor behind the short line before striking the opposite side wall. After hitting the second side wall, it should rebound parallel to the back wall.

Index

About the Authors

Ed Turner, PhD, is a professor in the Health, Leisure, and Exercise Department at Appalachian State University in North Carolina. He has taught racquetball at the university level since 1978 and racquet sports since 1964. His students have included top open racquetball players, such as Wiley Fisher, Jin Yang, and Eric Gentry.

In 1990 Turner received the North Carolina College Outstanding Physical Educator of the Year award. He has written numerous articles on racquetball strategy, and he's the coauthor of *Skills & Strategies for Winning Racquetball* and *Innovative Theory and Practice of Badminton.*

In addition to being an accomplished instructor, Turner is a top-rated open tournament racquetball player. He lives in Boone, NC.

Top-ranked International Racquetball Tour (IRT) pro **Woody Clouse** knows from first-hand experience what it takes to excel in the sport. As the lead instructor for the IRT, Woody is the best when it comes to helping other players excel too. He also serves as the media relations director for IRT.

A professional instructor since 1979, Clouse serves as consultant to the top professionals in the world. In 1987 he coached the Ecuadorian National Team. Clouse conducts racquetball clinics and seminars, and is the featured instructor for ESPN's Racquetball Show.

As a monthly contributor to *KILLSHOT Magazine,* Clouse shares his insights into the game and the strategies he learned from all-time racquetball greats like Bud Muelhieson and Cliff Swain.

He lives with his wife, Jacqueline, in Truckee, CA and enjoys hiking, surfing, and skiing.

Improve your game with these quality resources

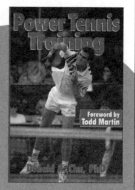